THE DIVER'S COMPLETE GUIDE TO EUROPE'S No.1 UNDERWATER CENTRE

FORT BOVISAND

by

KENDALL McDONALD

Although reasonable care has been taken in preparing this guide, the publishers and author respectively accept no responsibility or liability for any errors, omissions or alterations, or for any consequences ensuing upon the use of, or reliance upon, any information contained herein. Due caution should be exercised by anyone attempting dives on any site herein described or indicated.

The reproduction by any means in whole or part of any content of this book is expressly forbidden without the written permission of the author.

Front cover picture is by courtesy of the Western Morning News.

Rear cover photograph by Dave Peake is of a diver on the bow of the American Liberty ship, the James Eagan Layne, sunk in Whitsand Bay.

First published in 1997.
Published by Wreckwalker Books, Cradles Cottage, Thurlestone,
 Kingsbridge, Devon TQ7 3NE.
Copyright: Kendall McDonald 1997.
ISBN 0 9528637 1 5

Printed by E. J. Rickard Ltd. of Plymouth

Fort Bovisand is the most important dive centre in Europe, catering not only for thousands of amateur divers every year, but also running commercial diver courses, which provide the world's oil and salvage companies with properly-trained deep sea underwater experts.

Plymouth Ocean Projects Limited, the company which runs the Fort, also operates a highly-skilled civil engineering operation, whose divers carry out major work in many parts of the world.

The Fort on which all these operations are based is one of the finest surviving examples of the British defences against the threat of invasion by the French.

However, the Fort is, in fact, so well preserved that students of military history use it as a "living history textbook". Lecture rooms, photo labs, equipment stores, and accommodation for divers have all been fitted into the magazines and gun casemates with minimum disturbance to their original layout.

The immense number of diving courses of all kinds held at the Fort mean that there are few qualified divers working deep on undersea projects all over the world, who have not had the benefit of "diving Bovi". And there are few amateurs who have not at least one "Dived Bovisand" entry in their logbooks.

Today Fort Bovisand which can sleep over 100 divers at a time, continues to provide the diver, both amateur and professional, with everything he or she needs for hobby or career. Changes to diving techniques, new gas mixtures and the new equipment of the computer age are swiftly tested and adopted by the commercial diving courses based on the nearby Breakwater Fort in Plymouth Sound. The best of those advances are passed on to the amateurs, whose courses are run in such close proximity to the commercial diving at the Fort.

Fort Bovisand was opened in 1970 by Plymouth Ocean Projects Ltd. Its grounds cover nearly 13 acres. The Underwater Centre has classrooms with modern teaching aids for basic and advanced diver-training. At the Fort there is a fully-operational diving medical centre.

Underwater photographers are catered for at the Fort with a darkroom and large lecture room, fully equipped with 16mm cine, video, and 35mm slide projection facilities. There are drying rooms, multiple air charging outlets and hire and repair shops. A large training tank is used for first lessons in basic underwater cutting, welding and power tools. Twenty feet in diameter and 10ft deep, it can be used for basic scuba training by arrangement.

Bovisand Harbour belongs to the Fort and is the "gateway" to excellent and varied diving. The area of the harbour provides depths down to 10m and is sheltered by an L-shaped jetty of solid limestone blocks, topped with granite. This jetty acts as both an embarkation point for boats and a diving platform with a built-in air supply which can feed low-pressure air to six diving stations underwater in the harbour at the same time.

This book includes the story of Bovisand from Ice Age to present day. That story might well have ended in 1957, when the Ministry of Defence withdrew the remaining small contingent of troops. The last man out turned out the lights and locked the gates. The Fort was left on its own to fall down.

Occasionally, the Ministry of Defence, as custodians of the Fort, opened those gates, though it was easier to climb over the rubble at the sides. The men who were let in were prospective tenants - for a very short time! All of them shook their heads, appalled at the size of the problems, and the probable costs of conversion, and caught the next train out of Plymouth.

Two men, however, came more than once to look at the ruins. They too shook their heads like all the others, but on February 1st, 1970, with much misgivings, Alan Bax and Jim Gill signed a seven-year lease. Work, putting concrete on to their dream of the Fort as Britain's greatest watersports centre, started that very day.

Though those two men are still on the board of directors, the Fort now has new owners. The new lease-holders too have a dream of the Fort in the future. Their plans too are part of this book.

KENDALL McDONALD

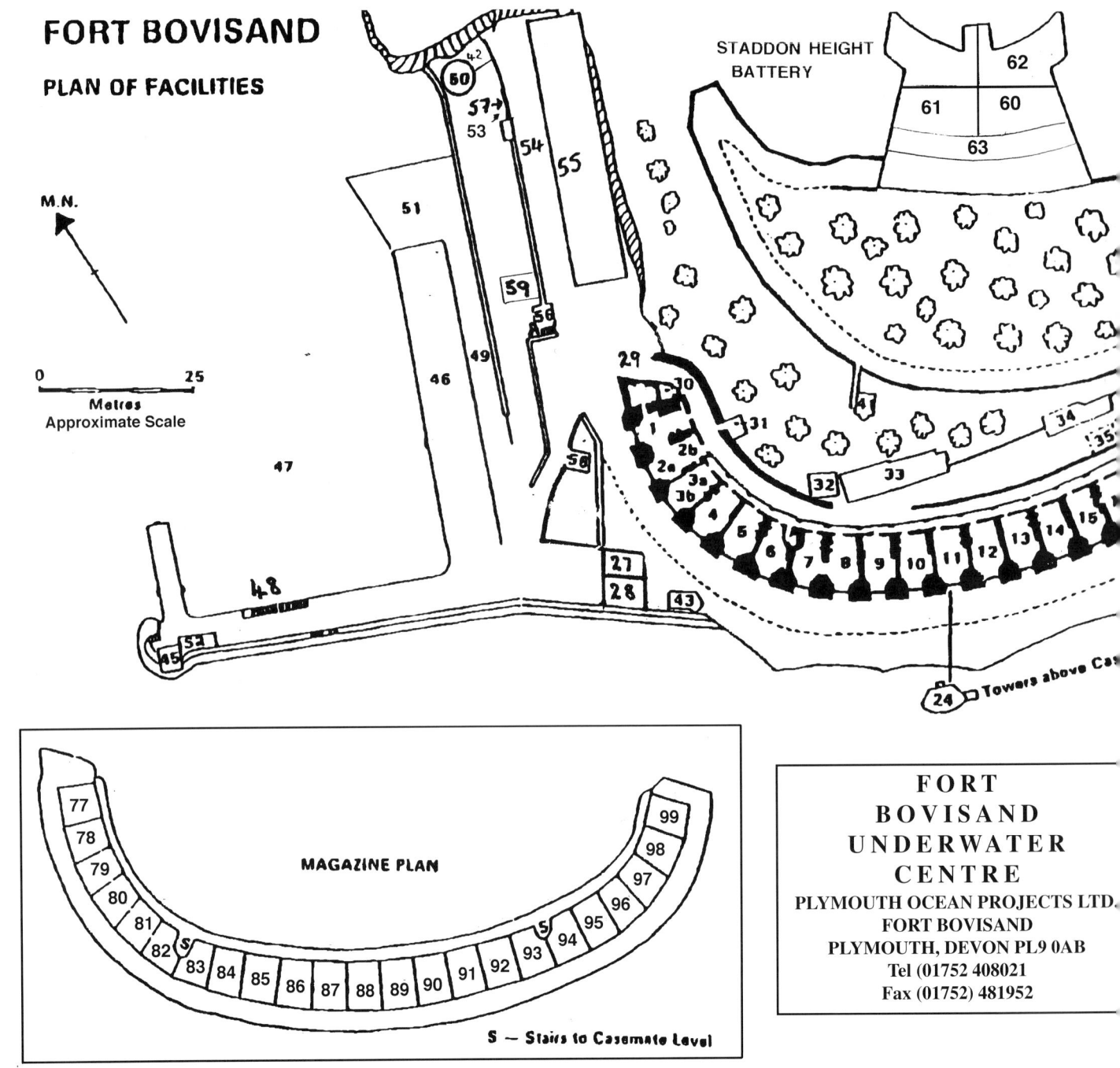

Key to map numbers:

1 to 3	Hire Centre and Store	42	Tank Diving Control Room
4	Shop	43	Instructors Changing Room
5	Changing Rooms	45	Diving Control Room
6	Classroom	46	RIB/Inflatable Park
7 & 8	Joint Service Sub Aqua Diving Centre (JSSADC) - Classroom & Offices	47	Harbour Diving Training Area
		48	Landing Steps
		49	Launching Slip
9	Men's Washroom	50	Diving Training Tank
10 & 11	Dormitories	51	Landing Apron
12	Reception	52	Ready Use Equipment Store
13 & 14	Dining Room	53	Training Offices
15	Kitchen	54	Residents Car Park
16 & 17	Conference Room	55	Accommodation Block
18 & 19	Dormitories	56	Outboard Store
20	Classroom	57	Medical Centre
21 to 23	JSSADC - Accommodation	58	Equipment Washing Area
24	Bar	59	Training Recompression Chamber
27	Harbour Cafe	60 to 62	Self Catering Accommodation
28	Workshop	63	4 x Twin bedded Rooms
29	Entrance		
30	Men's Toilet		**Magazines**
31	Compressor Room	77 to 79	Stores
32	Ladies Toilet	80	Classroom
33	Accommodation	81	Equipment Classroom
34	Administrative Offices	82	Darkroom
35	Drying Room	83	Store
36	Classroom	84 to 87	JSSADC Storerooms etc.
37	Laundry	88 to 94	Classrooms
38	Sailing School Office	95 to 98	Stores
41	Marine Engineering Contracts Office	99	Rigging Classroom

In the Beginning.

IF we could boldly go where no man has been before - aboard the Space Ship *Enterprise* at warp speed back to Bovisand's past, it is pretty certain that we would ask to be beamed back on board just as quickly as we had been transported down to Earth. For what we would find behind the time barrier would be pretty terrifying.

About 350 million years ago Plymouth Hoe was a coral reef. The sea was warm and so was the land. Somewhere near Drake's Island underwater volcanic eruptions turned the sea to steam and killed the coral. In the quiet between these eruptions the coral would grow again. We know that because geologists who examined a block of limestone taken from Pigeon Cave, Cattedown, discovered that there were at least 27 eruptions in the ocean nearby all those millions of years ago. Layers of ash showed in the limestone as thin gritty bands of red.

But that stone can't tell us anything more because the Devonian Period - some 405 to 345 million years B.C. - was a time of vast upheavals, pushing up the limestones and sandstones of Bovisand out of the warm shallow seas. Soon life seethed in those waters.

If we had been able to travel through time, this wouldn't have been the time to go for a swim! Imagine 50-foot long shark-like creatures in the water where the harbour is now. Creatures whose bodies were largely covered with plates of armour. At first these placoderms had to lift their whole skulls to open their mouths but within a short time as time goes, about 60 million years, they had adapted so that their jaws now had teeth for biting, paved jaws for crushing, and a pair of huge fins which steadied them for the kill.

These monsters shared the waters with 15-foot-long whelks and nine-foot sea scorpions. Beam me up, Scotty! But to be fair, no one at all amid the giant ferns of Bovisand was thinking about a dip - man, even in the most primitive form had millions of years to go before He and She were to be seen near Plymouth Sound.

In the meantime, we know from fossil finds that some 200 species of sharks were on the bite. Around 230 million years ago, the first crabs and lobsters appeared. Dinosaurs walked the slopes of Bovi about that time and became extinct 100 million years later.

The first men to reach Plymouth Sound were hunters, forced south by the Ice Age. The real ice never reached Bovisand, though it was of course bitterly cold. The glaciers seem to have come to a stop at what is now the North Devon coast. Early men took advantage of south-facing caves at Cattedown and lived there while hunting big game in the wooded valleys roundabout.

But even if there were no great glaciers covering Plymouth Sound, the sea had gone. The more ice the less sea. At one time the sea is thought to have been hundreds of feet below the present level. This would mean that when we were beamed down from *Enterprise* to stand with Spock on the top of the hill up

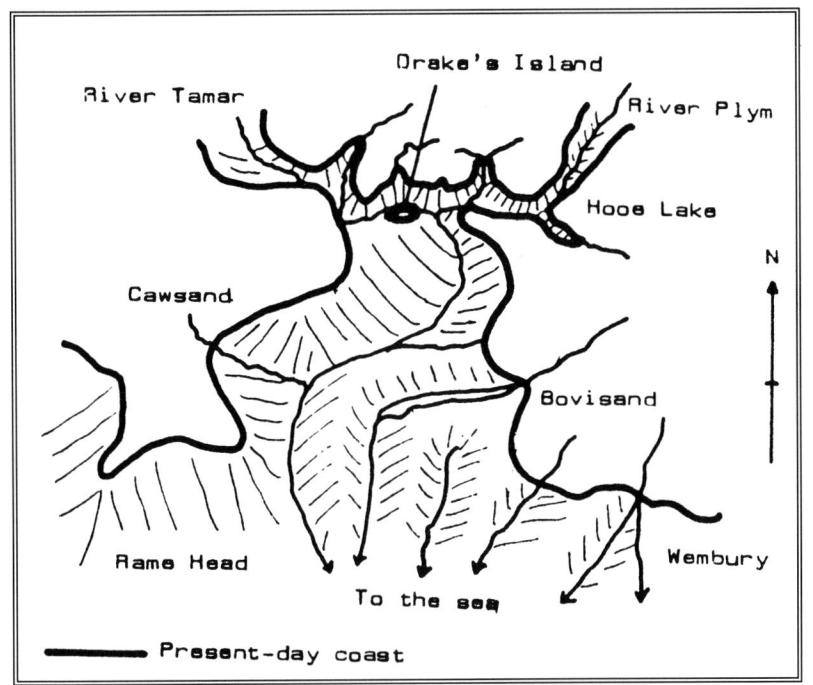

Plymouth Sound before the sea came back.

which the Fort sprawls today, there would be no sign of sea. The sea shore then was way out beyond Eddystone. The River Tamar and the Plym would have flowed out to the south-west between the **hills** of Eddystone and Hands Deep. The North Sea and the Dover Straits were dry land, making unimagineable any squabble about joining Europe!

If we had found ourselves on the top of Staddon Heights, courtesy of Captain Kirk's transporter room, we would be standing on grassland set among bare stretches of limestone "pavements". Below us as the hillside fell away to Staddon Point (the tip of Bovisand Pier today), the grassland would turn to scrub and right down where the sea is today would be a huge forest of birch and pine.(Divers today have found fossilised remains of this forest on the seabed out from the Fort.)

Faraway and out over the tops of the tall trees, we would just be able to pick out the hills of Eddystone some 14 miles away where the Tamar reached the sea. To our right, we would see the River Plym emerging from a limestone gorge near the Cattewater as it turned to the West to meet the Tamar. Both rivers were cutting deep channels through the earth so that their beds were 100 feet deeper than they are today. As the Tamar reached Barn Pool and Mount Edgcumbe, it was deflected by a ridge capped by a volcano. This today is Drake's Island.

The Tamar flowed around this knoll and picked up the waters of the Plym somewhere around the head of today's Mount Batten breakwater. From our vantage point we should be able to see the combined rivers passing through between two hills which are now the Mallard and Winter shoals on Admiralty charts. The valley the rivers cut between those two hills is now better known to sailors as "Smeaton Pass".

Next the Tamar-Plym ran straight towards us in a steep-sided gorge, then boiled as it hit a rock wall running out from Bovisand. The tips of that rock barrier used to be known to Plymouth mariners as the Panther, Shovel and St.Carlos Rocks before the Breakwater was built on top of them. Now the raging river was deflected even further to the west to gouge out today's Western Channel. It is fascinating to see that big ships of today heading for the Hamoaze and Devonport follow the ancient course of the Tamar all those millions of years ago - past the western end of the Breakwater, across and up the Sound to Smeaton Pass, cut through Drake's Channel, where the Tamar made its way round the volcano of Drake's Island, and so into the Hamoaze.

Nobody knows when man took to the waters of the Tamar. At this time it may have been much too fast running for him. We do know that he hunted along the hills and in the forests around Bovisand and Staddon and the opposite bank of the Tamar near Maker. Flint arrow-heads and spear-points prove that and piles of seashells, mostly mussels, mark his favourite picnic sites. But he was more a meat than fish man. Bones of elephants, rhinoceros, wolves, deer and hyaenas have been found by workmen around the caves at Fisons Quarry at Cattedown and at Oreston, which early man obviously called home.

But his happy hunting grounds disappeared when the sea came back in about 8,000 BC. It didn't happen overnight, but as the ice retreated to the sort of Artic and Antartic limits we know today, the sea crept up and over the ancient coastline.

They Called It Boye Sand.

So the sea came back, creeping up the deep gorges of the Tamar and Plym until Plymouth Sound as we know it today finally emerged. Drowned were the forests and even the wall of rock, which ran out from the present site of Fort Bovisand, was covered deeply enough to form today's Eastern Channel.

In time only the rocky tops of the original rock wall stuck up out of the sea and then as the waters rose even more, the Panther and the Shovel and St.Carlos rocks became dangerous shoals.

Though these shoals partially broke the violence of Southerly gales, when Man first took to the Sound there is evidence that he sheltered from such winds by going well up the Tamar or into the Cattewater and often even further up the Plym. Those southerly storms plagued the Sound for centuries to come. Though its waters looked like the perfect haven, sailors soon learned to anchor right up the rivers in any kind of bad weather.

Because the shipping did come. Though Britain was now an island, the narrow seas which cut us off from the rest of Europe were not a barrier for very long. Ships, probably flat-bottomed at first with skin sails, were sailing from Southern Spain to the West of England, Scotland and even Sweden, at the end of the British Neolithic period around 2,000 BC. This means they were here at the beginning of the Bronze Age.

Though so far no Bronze Age shipwreck has been found in Plymouth Sound, there was a Bronze Age settlement at Bilbury at the head of Sutton Pool. It was a defended place belonging to a chieftain called Billa. The men who built hut circles on Dartmoor came down from the Moor to this settlement and to other places on the Devon coast where they would trade the tin they mined with ships from France or possibly Spain.

The wreck of one of these tin traders has been found not far to the east of Plymouth in the mouth of the River Erme. Here divers were investigating a wreck of 1506, part of the fleet of Philip, King of Castile, when they found 42 crude ingots of almost pure tin close to Mary's Rocks, which form a deadly underwater barrier across the mouth of the estuary. This wreck is believed to be connected with the Bronze Age settlement on the shore at Bantham Ham, close to Burgh Island and the mouth of the River Avon. It might also explain the presence of another Bronze Age wreck even further to the east at Moor Sands, near Salcombe, from which divers have raised bronze swords and axeheads.

Inshore fishing boats were common around this time and as the Bronze Age merged into the Iron Age around 450BC, the flow of shipping in and out of the Sound increased dramatically. Finds on land during the construction of Fort Stamford, near Turnchapel, and the work on Mount Batten R.A.F. Station showed that Mount Batten and the surrounding area - though not quite as far along as Fort Bovisand - had been the sites of settlements from Iron Age to Roman times.

Divers recovering one of the tin ingots from the mouth of the Erme.

Mind you, any ancient ship captain might not have regarded Plymouth as very welcoming when he sailed in past Bovisand. For right ahead of him on the Hoe were two huge white figures. These giants were carved out of the grassland covering the white limestone and appeared to be wrestling with one another, even though one carried a huge club at the same time! These hill carvings were not destroyed until 1671.

We know all about them thanks to Geoffrey of Monmouth, who wrote it all down in the 12th century. He says they were Corineus and Gogmagog. Corineus was, according to Geoffrey, a Trojan hero who sailed to Devon after the sack of Troy and found the area around Plymouth occupied by a tribe of giants. Battle between the giants and Corineus's warriors was soon joined and was finally decided by a hand-to-hand battle between Corineus himself and the chief of the giants, Gogmagog. This man 'v' giant struggle took place on Plymouth Hoe.

It is hardly surprising that Gogmagog, being a bit bigger than Corineus, started off the bout well by breaking three of the Trojan's ribs. Corineus, as befits a man who gave his name to Cornwall, though hurt was not prepared to take this lying-down. Maddened by pain, he threw Gogmagog into the sea off the Hoe. To throw a giant that far is not quite such a feat as it sounds as anyone over six feet tall in those days was called a giant. Most of our forebears were inclined to be on the short side. But it was enough of a triumph for the victors to carve a memorial to the struggle on the Hoe.

The captains of the Roman galleys which were soon using the Hoe would have known that carving well during all the centuries that the Romans used Plymouth as a port. But in 410 A.D., Rome was threatened and the last of the recalled legions sailed home past Bovisand. Then was the time of the Saxons and the Normans. Plymouth as a town began to grow. But little happened to change the physical appearance of Bovisand, unless it was the growing number of ships which anchored off Bovisand Bay. The bay became one of the most important points for ships in the whole of Plymouth Sound. The reason for this was not the good anchoring qualities of the

This print dated 1724 of Plymouth Sound shows big ships anchored off Bovisand while waiting for water.

seabed, but the fact that a powerful clear stream of the best Devon water flowed down from the hillside to the shore (traces of that stream can be seen crossing the beach to this day).

The captains of ships of all kinds and of all ages knew that stream well. Drake, who was soon to turn the Spanish Armada's stately progression up the Channel into a rout, had known it since a boy. Hawkins, Frobisher, Howard, Grenville...name any seaman of the times and you name a man who had watered his ships at Bovisand.

Incidentally, it seems likely that there was a beacon flaring in the wind on Staddon Heights above Bovisand to warn of the Armada's coming, just one burning dot in the chain of fires which ran from headland to headland in 1588. As it burned, Drake finished his game of bowls on the Hoe.

Apart from Bovisand, the only other place in Plymouth Sound with such an easy supply of water was opposite at Cawsand. Otherwise water barrels had to be carried to the ships in tenders from Plymouth itself. But none of those great captains, or their seamen, would have understood you if you talked of "Bovisand". They called it "Boye Sand" and it seems likely that there were some permanent "boyes" in position just off the inlet where the stream ran out to sea. Ships would tie up to these buoys while their boats went ashore to fill the water casks.

There is some evidence that there was some sort of landing stage at the southern end of Bovisand Bay. I would have thought though that the men in charge of the watering party would have brought their boats as near the stream exit as the weather would allow, beaching if possible right in the mouth of the stream. For the casks of those days varied from the "baricos", cask made oval to prevent them rolling about at sea, and the "runlets" of a maximum size of 18 gallons and often used for cordials or brandies, via the "hogsheads" of 63 gallons, to the "pipes" of 126 gallons, and finally the monster "butts" of 140 gallons. It is unlikely that the larger water casks ever left the ship, being filled in position from the smaller ones brought out to the ship from shore.

If the idea of permanent buoys for ships in Bovisand Bay in Elizabethan times surprises you then you should read Captain John Smith's "A Sea Grammar" published in 1627. He writes: "To those Cables and Anchors belongs short peeces of wood called Boyes, or close hooped barrels like Tankards, as is said, but much shorter, to show you the Anchor....There is another sort of Cans called Can Boyes, much greater, mored upon shoules to give Marriners warning of the dangers". Perhaps the Tinker Shoal, such a danger in the Eastern Entrance route before the building of the Breakwater, held such a can buoy. Certainly in 1690, Bovisand Bay of today was marked on charts as "Bouy Sand"

From Boye Sand to Bovisand is not a long step. Try saying Boye Sand over and over again as quickly as you can and you can almost hear the name change!

In 1765 Benjamin Donn's map marks "Bovey Sand" with quite a big inlet clearly marked "Fresh Water". But whatever they called it, the use of Bovisand Bay as watering place went right on into the 1800s.

However, it was never used when the wind was from the South-South-West or when a Southerly gale or South-South-East wind was building up. The Sound at such times was no place to be caught out in open water. Ships that didn't seek shelter became yet another name on the horrendous list of ships wrecked inside the Sound.

No Sound Protection.

In earlier days, however, there were other dangers in the Sound than bad weather. The Turks penetrated right in to Plymouth seeking galley slaves and the seamen of Brittany were just as quick to loot. Their target was the old port, which is now Sutton Harbour. A chain boom across the mouth of the Harbour from Teat's Hill almost where the new lock gates are positioned seems to have had little deterrent effect.

But it was the sea itself that was the real enemy of Plymouth then. Growth was slower than in other West Country ports, such as Dartmouth. This may well have been due to the damaging onshore winds. Sheltering in the Cattewater from southerly winds was not the complete answer. Early reports say that so packed on such occasions was the Cattewater that the wind curled round Mount Batten Point and smashed the anchored ships into one another and many sank. "Cat" in early writings meant either a ship or a fort. Unless there was a Roman fort at Mount Batten, we must assume that Cattewater meant simply "Shipwater" which is a good name for a haven. Certainly the Kattegat or Cattegat means the "Shipgate" to the Baltic.

The fact that sheltering in the Cattewater didn't always save you was dramatically shown in June 1973 when a bucket dredger was stopped dead by striking some wreckage. Her bucket brought some ancient timber to the surface, which looked very like an old keelson. But there was not only wood in the dredger's bucket. There too were parts of two small wrought-iron breech-loading guns, dating to Tudor times. Divers led by Commander Alan Bax of Fort Bovisand raised the rest of the keelson and another gun as an underwater archaeology project. Further underwater work by archaeologist Dr.Mark Redknap is detailed in a report published by the National Maritime Museum.

But what ship was she? A search of Plymouth City archives found several strandings in the area between 1475 and 1575 and finally narrowed the field down to

The keelson of the Cattewater wreck.

the *St.James of the Croyne,* a trading ship lost "in great winds" in the night of January 17, 1494. Without furthere evidence no one can, of course, be certain that the wreck was of this ship, but a casualty of that sort of time she most certainly was.

The passing years had little effect on Bovisand, but momentous events sailed by. On September 6, 1620, for example, the 180-ton *Mayflower* went past and out to sea carrying the Pilgrim Fathers off to found a new settlement in Massachusetts, which they called Plymouth in memory of their last English port of call.

The Civil War of 1642 to 1646 brought warlike excitement to Bovisand. Plymouth stood for Parliament and was soon under siege by Royalists. The Royalists, having seen Cromwell's men break the siege from the sea in 1643, now patrolled the coast around the Sound. They were particularly alert at Bovisand to stop any attempt by Parliamentarian ships to land men behind the Royalist lines. The Royalists on such patrols knew only too well when they had lost the war - 300 cannon from Plymouth were fired out over the Sound to welcome Cromwell's victory!

In 1690, Plymouth was taken in another way. It was then that the Royal Navy decided that the town was to be the major naval base in the South-West. Their Lordships decision was surprising because of the winds which continued to plague the Sound. And their memories must have been short because everyone knew that on November 26, 1627, the Duke of Buckingham's fleet had been caught at anchor by a Southerly gale and huge winds had driven 15 ships ashore in the Hamoaze and wrecked another five in the Cattewater.

Perhaps no one in the Admiralty was old enough to remember that costly affair, but surely a series of gales in the autumn of 1689 should have made them hesitate about making Plymouth their major base. Then a 6-gun fireship, *Charles and Henry,* was sunk at the end of November. And on Christmas Day down went the 34-gun *Centurion* on Mount Batten and so did the 62-gun *Henrietta*.

It was hardly too late for them to change their mind when, only a year after making Plymouth their major port, the 90-gun *Coronation* was lost with over 300 men while trying to get to shelter in the Sound from a vicious South-South-East gale, which also drove other men o'war ashore. (The loss of *Coronation* is detailed in the wreck sites later in this book).

It is almost impossible to believe that at this time no one raised the question of building a breakwater to stop further casualties. But if they did it is not recorded. The first written record of such a plan is dated 1788. It was put forward officially by Mr. William Smith, then the Master-Attendant of Devonport Dockyard, and was promptly and totally rejected.

The trouble with Mr. Smith's plan was that he thought too big. His idea was to build a great breakwater from Staddon Point (where Fort Bovisand's harbour is today) out to Panther Rock in the middle of the entrance to the Sound. It seems that the powers that were glanced at the plan, turned straight to the costings, turned white at the figure they saw, and turned it down on the spot. They had, of course, no idea how much the real thing was to cost them later on! Mr. Smith's plan was filed and forgotten - until the *Dutton* was wrecked in 1796.

The *Dutton,* a 760-ton East Indiaman, had been on her way to the West Indies for several weeks when she ran into appalling weather and started leaking so badly that Captain Sampson turned back for Plymouth. Conditions on board were terrible for the *Dutton* was being used as a troopship and was carrying over 500 men of the Queen's Second Regiment and their families below decks as well as a large number of civilian passengers in better accommodation.

The ship was low in the water when she reached the entrance to Plymouth Sound. Unfortunately, a Southerly gale decided to arrive at the same time. Captain Sampson ran for the shelter of the Cattewater. But didn't make it. The *Dutton* struck the

Mount Batten Shoal, which ripped off her rudder. Though all her sails were down, the huge wind on her masts was enough to send her careering across the mouth of Cobbler Channel and to pile her on to the rocks in front of the Hoe, near the Citadel. Her masts crashed down adding to the panic on board.

But the panic was not confined to the landlubbers among the passengers and the troops. To their eternal shame, the ship's officers managed to get a line ashore, tied their end to the broken mainmast, and pulled themselves ashore leaving the rest to their fate.

Huge crowds gathered on the Hoe, but just stood and watched as the ship started to break up in front of them. None of those watchers made the slightest attempt at rescue and were prepared to stand and see all aboard perish at their feet.

There is no doubt that all left on the ship would have died if it had not been for one man. Sir Edward Pellew, captain of *HMS Indefatigable*, who was on shore at the time, rushed to the scene. After all his efforts to muster the crowds into a rescue attempt had failed, he set off alone along the rope to the ship, which the officers had used for their escape. But before he did so, he sent a messenger to his own ship ordering her boats to the scene.

The rope from the shore to the fallen mainmast involved Sir Edward in swinging round the stump of the mast as he boarded the ship. As he did so, he injured his back, but managed to take command and restore some sort of order to the panic-stricken mob aboard. He is said to have seized a sword and used it to enforce his orders! The boats from *Indefatigable* managed to get alongside and despite the huge seas took off large numbers of the troops. On the other side of the ship, Sir Edward rigged up some sort of ropeway to the shore and more people escaped by that route.

In all, Sir Edward's efforts resulted in over 600 people being saved from the ship. Only 15 lives were lost. Sir Edward was made a Freeman of Plymouth for his efforts and later became Viscount Exmouth.

The loss of the *Dutton*, where thousands could see it and so close to the shore, raised a great public outcry - not just against the officers who had been such cowards, but in favour of some form of protection being given to the shipping which used Plymouth and the Sound. The idea of a breakwater was heavily supported. Mr Smith's plan was revived. Local dignitaries lobbied the Government and the Navy to do something.

Build a Breakwater! That was the popular cry. But as far as the merchants of Plymouth were concerned it was not without a good deal of self-interest. Even without a breakwater, shipping in the Sound was booming. Just think how many more ships would use the port of Plymouth if it could be made safer.

Plymouth was a base for the Indiamen. It was, as it always had been, a base for privateers. During the Napoleonic wars it was to Plymouth that they brought their prizes. But it was all very well capturing a prize, putting aboard a prize crew, and bringing her safely back to Plymouth, if she was going to be sunk at the very last in the Sound itself by the weather.

In 1803, for example, the privateers had done so well that there was scarcely room for one more ship in the Cattewater, to which shelter every prudent captain brought his prize. Plymouth merchants were delighted with the extra cash this brought them. But they weren't so happy when, as happened regularly, some of those prizes were sunk within sight of the Hoe. So the clamour for a breakwater grew and grew. If it was to cost a lot of money, no matter. The sums involved in prize money were not trifling either.

In January, 1805, Captain Halsted of the *Phoenix* brought the Spanish *El Mercurio* into the Sound. She carried some 20,000 silver dollars and gold dust weighing 300 ounces. In February, *Polyhemus* brought in the *Santa Gertruda*. Her cargo included 1,500,000 silver dollars. And in March that same year, the *Flying*

Pallas brought in another Spaniard with diamonds, gold and silver bars and coins worth over £1,000,000.

Those men who had joined the 36-gun *Pallas* the previous autumn after reading posters put up around Plymouth by her captain Lord Cochrane asking men to join him in ambushing the "galleons of La Plata Fleet from Cartagena" were able to retire on their cut of that voyage alone! Cochrane, who captured over 50 French and Spanish ships in his time, never needed to put up posters for crewmen again!

With those sorts of prizes vulnerable to sea and wind, it is no wonder that the demand for a breakwater became irresistable. Even so, it is difficult to allocate the driving seat to any one man. Lord Howick, First Lord of the Admiralty in 1806, is said to have been the man who ordered a survey. And Admiral Earl St.Vincent was pushing hard.

St.Vincent was a great man for the defence of the Realm. So his main interest was not the safety of the merchant ships, but in defending Britain against seaborne attack. To do that he needed a safe harbour for the Navy. He said: "I see no other chance of resisting the insatiable ambition of the ruler of France (Napoleon), but by making Plymouth Sound a secure mole at any expense".

What Breakwater?

MOLE or breakwater, call it what you will, was very much a matter of expense. Hundreds of thousands of pounds in those days as the estimated cost of a breakwater would be millions and millions in today's terms. But with St.Vincent prodding them into action, the Admiralty ordered a survey in 1806. Engineer John Rennie and the Master Attendant of Woolwich Dockyard, Joseph Whidbey, were given the task.

It is interesting to note that Whidbey, who had been sailing master of *Discovery* in the 1792 exploration of the Pacific, was chosen even though the Master Attendant of Devonport Dockyard had put forward a scheme in 1788. Though that scheme had been rejected out of hand, one would have thought that the man on the ground might have known a little more that an import from Woolwich a few years later. But Whidbey was to prove useful in more ways than one.

As soon as the news of the survey spread, the political objections flowed in. Captain Manderson of Falmouth was one of the loudest objectors. He suggested that Falmouth was a better place. His interest became plain when he pointed out that the Navy should move their dockyards to Falmouth where he just happened to be deeply involved in property!

The political uproar and the battle between Plymouth and Falmouth for the Navy's custom was considerably damped down when the current Master Attendant of Plymouth Dockyard, Mr.William Hemans, was invited to assist the survey. Mr.Hemans was the acknowledged expert on the strange flows and tides in the Sound. The three men worked fast. In April 1808, their report was ready. And on the 21st of that month it was presented to the Admiralty.

It was a very fine and swift piece of work. During the course of their work they had to examine many serious - and many crackbrained - ideas. Two of the schemes they had to consider seriously were:

(1) That 117 triangular floating frames of wood should be laid over the danger area, the Panther, Shovel and St.Carlos Rocks and other shoals in the centre of the Sound. These frames, 60 feet long by 30 feet wide, would be moored in position by chains and would break up the great swells sweeping into the Sound which did so much damage to anchored ships. The cost was a great attraction - a mere £200,000.

(2) To sink on the same shoals 140 wooden or stone towers in a double line and then to connect these towers with a superstructure so that they formed an open-arched mole similar to those of ancient Tyre and Athens. These towers were designed to be 50 feet high and have six-foot thick walls. Once on site they were to be filled with stone and sunk in position. This scheme had the advantage that it was strongly supported by General Bentham, who was the Civil Architect and Principal Surveyor of the Navy.

Marble bust of John Rennie.

It says much for the independence of Rennie and Whidbey that they rejected both schemes., particularly the second, but it may also explain why their report was left dormant for the next five years!

Their report also rejected, after more serious consideration: Plan A, which was to construct a pier out into the Sound from Penlee Point, close to the grave of part of *Coronation* (see Wreck sites). This breakwater was to be 1,000 yards long, 60 feet high and 150 feet wide at its base. It would certainly shelter Cawsand Bay, but Rennie and Whidbey considered that it might lead to silting up of the Sound and would certainly increase the swell in the Sound by restricting its entrance. The expense of building in the 10 fathoms of water off the Point was also a drawback.

Then they looked at Plan B, which concentrated on the other side of the Sound, the Bovisand side. This involved another breakwater running from Staddon Point (where the Fort is now) out to Panther Rock, a distance of 2640 yards. It was, in fact, Smith's plan of 1788. Once again it was thought that it might lead to silting and would restrict the entrance for big ships.

The same doubts arose from Plan C, which was another breakwater running out from Andurn, Point a headland to the South of Bovisand Bay. It was shorter than the others and ran out to Shovel Rock, a distance of 1700 yards.

Andurn Point was also the land base for Plan D, yet another breakwater. This time it was to run for 2,900 yards to Panther Rock. But Rennie and Whidbey felt that it, too, would cause silting.

Finally they came down decisively in favour of one idea: "A detached mole should be formed at the mouth of the Sound, where nature pointed out the site for such an erection by a string of shoals called the Panther, Shovel and St.Carlos Rocks, on each side of which the channel is deep and sufficiently wide to afford safe passage for vessels".

Rennie added that the construction of the mole or breakwater should be of "rubble or rough angular blocks of stone, from two to ten tons weight and upwards, mixed with smaller materials, cast into the sea, when the waves would arrange them in the shape best calculated to resist the action of the breakers". In this way, the shoals in the centre of the Sound were to be raised to a height "sufficient to arrest the undulation of the sea".

The mole itself was to consist of three arms, "or kants", inclining towards each other at an angle of 120 degrees; thus giving the structure a curved form, which it was considered would prevent "the too great accumulation of the waves on the outside and offer the least impediment to the current". The planned length was 1,700 yards and it was to be raised to the level reached by mean half-tide.

Then came the crunch. The cost was estimated to be £1,055,200 because the amount of stone required would be 2,000,000 tons. Not surprisingly, the answer to this expensive proposal by the Admiralty was complete and utter silence.

Rennie's Rampart.

THAT silence was to last for five years. But the Admiralty finally cracked under continued pressure from their own admirals who repeatedly reported that the Sound was a dangerous anchorage. They went further and underlined their dislike of Plymouth by using Torbay for the Fleet whenever possible.

However, "Rennie's Rampart" finally came to life on the 22nd of June, 1811. That was the date when the order for the construction of the Breakwater was approved by the Prince Regent's Privy Council. A few days later, John Rennie and Joseph Whidbey were given the go-ahead and asked to produce detailed (and fully costed) plans for the Admiralty, who expected the work to provide them with a sheltered mooring for "upward of fifty sail of the line".

First step was to secure the enormous quantity of stone that would be needed. Local limestone was an obvious choice. The best quarry for a supply of suitably dense stone was on the estate of the Duke of Bedford at Oreston, a mile up the Plym in the Cattewater. Twenty-five acres of the stone was leased from the Duke for £10,000. A price of one shilling and tenpence per foot was agreed for the rough stone. Any granite facing was to be paid for at the rate of two shillings and eightpence per foot.

In March 1812, work started. The quarries were opened with rails for trucks to move the stone down to specially built wharves. Ten sailing barges of 80 tons each were adapted to carry the stone out to the site.

The Breakwater from the west in 1829. A ship waits for water off Bovisand in the background. Note the stone-carrier boat on the left.

These ten stone-carriers were fitted with rails on their decks so that the really large blocks of stone could be run straight on board at the wharves after being pulled down from the quarry by horses. Rail tracks on board ships were not new - Smeaton had used them when building his Eddystone lighthouse.

There were another 45 smaller ships, described as sloops, to carry smaller stones. The operation of dumping these stones on the shoals was soon down to a fine art. It took exactly 50 minutes to moor and discharge the stone in the right place before the sloop was away for another load.

On August 12, 1812 - the Prince Regent's birthday - the first and centre stone was laid on the Shovel Rock. The water over the shoals varied from 50 to 60 feet. On March 30, the following year, the dumped stones broke surface for the first time at low water on the Spring tide. Some 43,789 tons of stone had been needed to do it.

However much small shipping in Plymouth was concentrated on building the Breakwater, other ships were entering and leaving the Sound on even more important and deadly work. Britain was in the process of beating Napoleon on land and at sea and at the same time fighting a futile war against America. The fact that none of this was allowed to interfere with the Breakwater work shows how highly the operation was regarded by the Admiralty.

The Lords of the Admiralty had another worry in Plymouth. The arrangements for water to be supplied to warships by filling barrels at Bovisand and Cawsand was proving more and more difficult. The stream at Cawsand, though the bigger of the two, was now being largely used to supply villages on the Rame peninsula. What had been good enough for the smaller ships of Drake was not sufficient for the huge ships of the Napoleonic wars. No Admiral could be happy if his ships had to queue up and be out of action for hours, if not days. Supposing the French caught them at such a time!

So the Navy called on John Rennie once again. Though they knew he was hard at work on the Breakwater, they asked him to design a new system for the water supply of Bovisand Bay. With difficulty, Rennie found time in early 1814 to submit a plan to the Admiralty, but heard nothing from them.

By August 1813, the Breakwater was far enough advanced for men to work on its surface. However, in March 1814, the sea put the plan to its first real test. A southerly gale sent huge seas sweeping into the Sound and crashed them against the stones. The unfinished structure absorbed all that force. So much so that a large three-decker rode out the storm in its shelter. Even so, Rennie and Whidbey decided to raise the height of the mole making it two feet above the high-water mark of Spring tides.

By the 11th of August, 1815, they were delighted to find that they had 1,100 yards showing above water and the speed of dumping seemed to get faster and faster.

In the world outside the Sound, Napoleon had escaped from Elba, but the Battle of Waterloo had been fought and won. Napoleon was on his way to exile in St.Helena as a prisoner on board *H.M.S.Bellerophon,* when she anchored in the Sound behind the Breakwater in October,1815.

The 74-gun, third-rate *Bellerophon* soon became one of Plymouth's first tourist attractions - boatmen made a small fortune taking people out to the ship to see the man who had kept Britain at war for almost 22 years. Though there was no guarantee that Napoleon would be seen, occasionally a small figure on the quarter deck in a green tunic with a red sash would appear on the quarter-deck. There is no record to say that he noted the inefficiency of the watering arrangement for the warships of his captors, but he must have seen the water tenders plying back and forth before he was sailed away to exile in the South Atlantic.

The war was over, but the Admiralty did not forget their water-supply problems. Rennie's plan was accepted and work started in 1816. Basically, his plan was to create a reservoir, which would be fed by the stream which poured out into the Sound in Bovisand Bay. From this reservoir the water was to be piped down a nine-inch cast-iron pipe to Staddon Point. To enable ships to water properly, Rennie planned a wharf 200 feet long with a jetty 70 feet long whose outer end would be in 12 feet of water at low Springs. This meant that the largest tenders and boats from the men o'war could come alongside at all states of the tide and take on water.

The wharf and jetty are still part of Bovisand Harbour today. Rennie's Reservoir is still there too - in a valley three-quarters of a mile from the shore and some 52 feet above high-water mark. At the front it is 150 feet wide, narrowing to 75 at the other end. It was 23 feet deep and was designed to hold 12,000 tuns or barrels. A tun was 252 gallons, the equivalent of two "pipes".

The reservoir today has shrubs and trees growing in it, but is in comparatively good condition. It holds water and it is not difficult to see how it could supply enough to meet the Admiralty requirement - to supply 50 ships of the line. "Fifty ships" seems to have been a magic number for the Navy Board of that time. This number is, you will recall, exactly the same number of ships that Rennie's Rampart was expected to shelter.

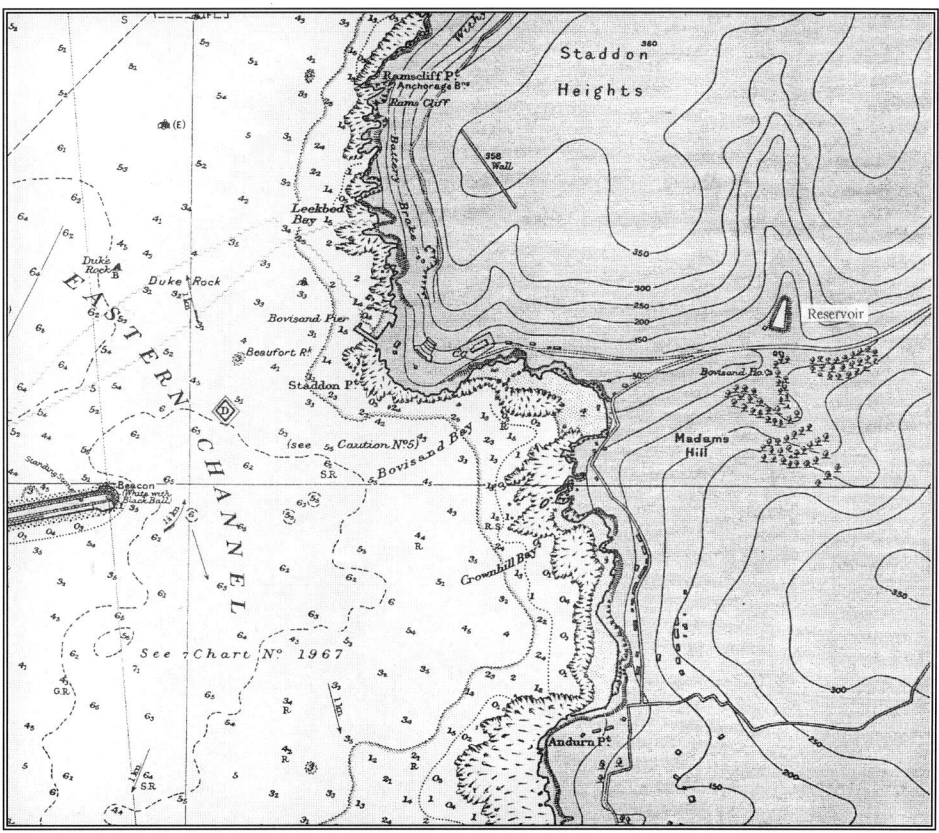

This old chart shows the position of Rennie's reservoir.

The jetty along which so many divers have walked, was built at the end of the pipeline using dressed limestone, which also came from the quarries at Oreston. The coping is of granite and that came from Dartmoor. The whole water project was completed in 1824 and cost £39,800.

Work on the Breakwater never stopped. By 1816 some 332,407 tons of stone was in position. Things were going well. Too well. On January 18, 1817, a strong southerly gale increased in the afternoon to hurricane force. Two hundred yards of the upper rubble on the Breakwater was ripped off and thrown by the sea right over the mole. Individual blocks followed. Two Navy ships, *H.M.S. Jasper*, a sloop, and *H.M.S. Telegraph*, a schooner, which had anchored outside the Breakwater, were wrecked.

The *Jasper* went ashore on Mount Batten with the loss of 65 lives including 15 women. The *Telegraph* was smashed right across the Sound ending up on the Hoe, but had only one casualty.

That night there were many other losses in the Sound, but even so the general opinion was that the Breakwater had taken a great deal of the sting out of the hurricane.

Some good came of that hurricane however. Rennie and Whidbey learned a lesson from the damage which the storm waves had done to their work - a lesson which was to save many lives later on. Looking at the damaged stonework, the two men realised that force of the sea had made a natural slope by tearing away some of the stones. But the great waves that had followed the height of the storm did no more damage after that. The two men had originally planned the slope of the south-facing side of the Breakwater, which would be directly opposed to the main force of the waves, to be 3:1. The hurricane had obviously not liked this and had flattened it to 5:1 or 11 degrees. So Rennie and Whidbey decided to give way to nature and kept the slope of the wall at that angle during the rest of the building.

Rennie was an absolute workaholic. In addition to other work, he designed the Royal William Victualling Yard at Stonehouse, though it was not to be built until 1824-35 by his son, Sir John Rennie. (The Yard covered 14 acres and is the largest engineer-designed building in Britain.)

John Rennie died in 1821, but Whidbey continued to supervise the Breakwater work. He lived in Bovisand House (it is called Bovisand Lodge today and is up behind the caravan park of Bovisand Bay). From the house he could look down on the Breakwater and he kept a close eye on it with the help of several telescopes.

The Admiralty, however, felt that this supervision was too much for one man and called in Sir John Rennie, Rennie's son, to help. The work went on apace - at the peak of the building 765 men were employed on it - but storms washed away segments almost as soon as they were completed. Repairs were carried out as soon as the sea allowed and the speed of repairs overtook that of the damage. The Breakwater continued to grow.

In fact, the Breakwater rising out of the sea and getting higher month by month became one of the sights of the West Country. Dignitaries of all kinds paid visits to it - when the sea was calm! One block on the paving of the top marks a very special visit. It is carved with the words: Prince Wm. Henry, Duke of Clarence, Duchess of Clarence, July 17th, 1827.

So the merchants of Plymouth had their breakwater, but they now had another worry. The Breakwater rose like an uncharted reef from the sea and presented yet another hazard to shipping. The Mayor was so worried that he wrote to the Admiralty about it and demanded that the original plan should be implemented. This plan had made provision for two lighthouses on the Breakwater, one at each end. Some sort of light did exist at western end for some years, but something more visible and more permanent was needed.

The lighthouses were a long time coming. In fact, Joseph Whidbey died in 1835 and the permanent lighthouse for the western end was not in place then. Work on it did not start until 1841. The light on the 126-ft high tower did not beam out until 1844, when the Breakwater was officially regarded as completed. Users of the channel at the eastern end had to be content with a coal beacon on a circular tower. It also had a refuge for shipwrecked sailors.

The John Murray guidebook for travellers in Devon and Cornwall, first published in 1859, describes that like this: "The E. of the Breakwater is constructed

The Breakwater from the air.

with a circular head, and of solid masonry, like the W., and supports a pyramidal beacon of beautiful white granite, 25 feet in height from the top of the Breakwater, and of 25 ft.diam. It is divided into 12 steps and crowned by a pole of African oak 17ft.high, supporting a hollow globe of gun-metal, in which the shipwrecked mariner may take refuge".

By the time the Breakwater was finished, 3,500,000 tons of stone and rubble had been used, more stone than is in the Great Pyramid of Egypt!

The French are Coming!.

BIG guns have played a major role in the history of Plymouth. The town was often under attack or more often threatened with it. So it is not surprising that the townspeople always had defence in mind. They did have good reason to worry.

Plymouth was twice plundered and burnt by the French in the wars of the 14th and 15th centuries. By the time Elizabeth the First came to the throne the need for defence was even more urgent for the town was already the chief naval arsenal in the land. When it was clear that the Spanish Armada planned an assualt on England, the Queen sent orders that the defences of Plymouth - obviously a prime target - were to be strengthened. In particular, more guns were to be set up on St.Nicholas Island, which we know today as Drake's Island. Other guns were placed to protect the rest of the Sound.

Though the Armada sailed past Plymouth, by the time of Cromwell's England Plymouth had ten demi-cannon, 49 culverin, six 12-pounders, 55 demi-culverin, 23 8-pounders, six 6-pounders, 25 sakers, 28 minions, seven 3-pounders and five falconets. When you know that a demi-cannon's weight was 4,000 lbs, a culverin 4,840lbs, a demi-culverin 3,400, a saker 1,400, a minion 1050 and a falconet 500lbs, you are looking at a huge firepower.

By the Peace of Utrecht in 1713, the Plymouth defences mounted 300 big guns, but after the war economies were inevitable, and there were plans to reduce the Plymouth guns to a mere 70.

There was the usual panic to restore the cuts in these coastal defences when war started again in 1778, first with France and then with Spain and Holland joining in shortly afterwards. But the years of neglect had done enormous damage - shot had flaked and swollen so that it wouldn't got into the muzzles, carriages had rotted and collapsed and great stores of powder were sodden and useless.

There was a right old panic in the Plymouth area. Spies in France reported that a French landing to start the invasion of England was likely in Cawsand Bay. New batteries were set up at Eastern King, West Hoe, Passage Point, Stonehouse Bridge, Cavalier Battery, and Lower Mount Wise. These were to supplement the guns at the Citadel, Mount Wise, Western King and Drake's Island.

At the same time another battery was built which led to the fortification of the Bovisand area. An open earth rampart was thrown up on Staddon Heights, just below the crest on the 350 foot contour line, and ten 12-pounders were installed. The exact date of this first Bovisand battery being ready for firing is not recorded, but it was there in the late 1770s and appeared then in Board of Ordnance reports.

There is no record of this new battery firing a shot in anger, but the big scare of August, 1779, had every gunner at his post for at least four days. The reason for this was the appearance of the French and Spanish fleets, 88 ships in all, off the Sound. At the same time the British fleet was out at sea, and the two enemy fleets were masters of the Channel.

The French had no idea that Plymouth lay before them almost completely defenceless. So defenceless that the Commissioner of the Dockyard sent a message to the Admiralty: "Shall I burn His Majesty's Dockyard or wait until the French Admiral comes in and does it?" While he waited for a reply, the dockyard workers were trained to handle the guns and prepared for a last-ditch stand.

The weather, however, was on the English side and a violent easterly gale forced the French and Spanish ships to run for shelter. Only after they had gone did the Commissioner get word from the Admiralty - not to be in so much of a hurry!

The guns of the coastal artillery changed little over the following years. Until, in fact, the coming of the Industrial Revolution which ushered in the world of steam-powered and armoured ships with rifled guns. Until then the targets of coastal guns were all sailing ships, which generally moved slowly and needed the wind to move at all.

The ranges of guns were short. Those new 12-pounders at Staddon Heights had an extreme range of 1800 yards. Which meant that shot could not reach the centre of the Sound where the Breakwater is today, but could command the Eastern Channel. The bigger guns on Maker Heights, across the Sound - four 32-pounders, six 24-pounders and 32 18-pounders could command the Western Channel with extreme ranges of 2,900, 2,700, and 2,600 yards respectively.

This time the end of hostilities did not mean the usual economies. Not as far as the defence of harbours such as Plymouth was concerned. Everyone had learned the lesson that Britain's coastal defences were sadly lacking and, surprisingly, proposed to do something about it.

The report of the Committee of Harbour Defences was produced on October 23, 1844. The members of the Committee were Captain Sir Thomas Hastings of the Royal Navy, Colonel Sir George Host, K.C.B. of the Royal Engineers and Lieutenant-Colonel Mercer of the Royal Artillery.

One of their many recommendations was that a permanent Fort or Battery should be erected to replace the earthworks at Staddon Heights.

They further recommended that the sum of £15,787, 12 shillings and ten pence three farthings should be voted for this work. It is an amazing costing right down to the three-farthings. But more amazing the money was made available.

As a result, the first granite stone was laid on October 18, 1845. Fort Bovisand was born!

The Fort – Mark One.

If you stand at the end of Rennie's Wharf, that is on the protecting outside wall of Bovisand harbour and look back up at the Fort, the place that first stone was laid lies right under the topmost building - a building that was very different to the one you see today. For a start it had towers on the east and west sides.

The Fort was originally designed to house 3 officers, 90 men and its armament was to be twelve 18-pounder guns. The whole idea of building up so high was to increase the range of the guns. The first real work followed straight after the laying of the foundation stone and it was finished on November 11, 1847. Eleven days later it was fully occupied.

As building forts go, it was a remarkably swift job. And even the cost had been kept below the estimate. The final accounts showed the total cost as £13,782, 12 shillings and seven pence.

Victoria had become Queen in 1837 and it was one of her A.D.Cs, a Colonel Oldfield, C.R.E. Western Division, who had been in overall charge of the work. In fact, he must have been pleased with the speed of the building because a tablet bearing his signature, confirming the dates, was placed in the lower room of the West Tower after the official commissioning ceremony at the Fort.

The finished construction was in three tiers or steps, coming down the hillside. The towers were on the bottom level. They were linked together by a rampart wall which was hollow but filled in with loose stone for strength in the places were storage rooms were not required. The stone filling was heaviest at each end of the rampart near the towers and in the exact centre portion of the wall.

The smooth-bore guns were on carriages on the "terreplein", which in the language of forts and artillery was the upper surface of the rampart. Today that is a terrace below private living accommodation, which occupies the highest portion of the Fort and is the old officers' quarters.

The whole structure as surrounded by a dry ditch, cut into the rock. Caponieres, another fort user word meaning a covered passage across the ditch of a fortified place, were on each flank of the work. One of the caponieres of the old Fort can be seen today down towards the seaward end of the great ditch. This caponiere allowed the defenders to fire along the ditch at anyone trying to cross it. Another can be seen high up the ditch near the top of the hill. They turned the ditch into a killing ground and one shudders to think of the massacre which would have taken place if anyone had tried to storm the fort that way!

The emphasis on defence to landward as well as seaward side was based on experience in the Napoleonic wars in Spain and Portugal - those attacking a fort from the sea knew they had little chance of success using their ships' guns in a frontal seaborne assault and so often attacked overland from the rear in a flanking move. It is this fear of land attack which explains many of the ditches and passageways you find as you wander around inside Bovisand. Defence in depth.

So the Fort which was known as the Staddon Height Battery and never as the fort which it really was, sat in splendour on the hillside for year after year. Though in the Fort the routine altered little; outside its ramparts, the world was changing fast.

The Navy started experiments with steam engines in its ships in 1833. By the time of the Crimean War in 1854 many ships were driven by steam, though the great wooden men o'war were still the major floating gun-platforms.

These wooden giants were on their last sea-legs due to the perfection of the hollow shell filled with explosives. Any one who doubted this had only to see what the Russian coastal batteries at Sebastopol did to Britain's wooden warships.

However, it is not fair to say that the Staddon Height Battery was completely cut off from the world. It was one of the few forts equipped with Anderson's Cupola device for preparing Martin's Liquid Iron Shells. Though that sounds very mysterious, the cupola and the shells were really an improved version of the old-time red-hot shot. In earlier days they had heated up shot in a cupola or furnace and then having rammed home the powder down the gun barrel and followed it with a wet wad, they tipped the glowing cannon-ball into the muzzle, and fired at once. The idea was to start a fire in the enemy ship and if the ball flew true, it usually suceeded. However, Martin's method, started in 1855, used a hollow round shot, lined with an insulating mixture of loam and cowhair. Anderson's Cupola was a portable blast-furnace which was set up near the guns and used to melt pig-iron. When the target came in range, one of Mr.Martin's patent shells was filled with molten iron. The portion at the filling hole solidified almost at once, making its own seal. When the shell hit the target, it broke up, molten iron flew all over the place, starting a mass of fires.

Bovisand's commander, like the others who had this equipment dumped on them, was not enthusiastic about its use. His main objection was against having a machine full of red-hot coke and molten iron in the middle of his gun battery and close to quantities of gunpowder! Mr.Martin's shells became obsolete in 1869, largely because of the impossibility of adapting them to the rifled guns which came into use before that date.

However, using the cupola was one of the few excitements to disturb the Staddon Height Battery in all those years. But even a fort tucked away on a hillside well away from the town could not remain unchanged for ever. Nor miss the growth of war-like exchanges at a diplomatic level with the French. By 1857, we were at loggerheads with the French, but not actually at war even if exchanging some pretty war-like words.

These words got even tougher when the French Navy stole a march on the Royal Navy by laying down a whole fleet of iron-clad ships in 1858. When the French Navy got even more iron-clads soon after the first deliveries, the whole of the Royal Navy's wooden walls became obsolete almost overnight.

Coast defence now became vitally important. While the Navy hastened to catch up with this new breed of warships, invasion scares swept the country. As usual in such circumstances the British changed their Prime Minister. Lord Palmerston was brought back! To calm public fears, he did what many a Prime Minister has done before - and after! He ordered the setting up of a Royal Commission. Its brief was "to consider the defences of the United Kingdom with special reference to Portsmouth, Plymouth, Portland, Pembroke, Dover, Chatham and Medway".

That commission's final recommendations would have a massive effect on Staddon Heights and would create Fort Bovisand as we know it today.

The Royal Commission was formally appointed by

Sidney Herbert, Secretary of State for War, on August 20, 1859. The members were Major-General Sir Henry David Jones of the Royal Engineers, Major-General Duncan Alexander Cameron, Rear-Admiral George Eliot, Major-General Sir Frederick Hallett, Captain Astley Cooper-Key of the Royal Navy, Lieutenant-Colonel John Henry Lefroy of the Royal Artillery, and Mr. James Ferguson representing the Treasury.

The reasons given for appointing the Commission were: "The introduction of rifled ordnance which has created a revolution in the practice of artillery and the introduction of steam which has revolutionised the state of naval warfare".

The members of the Commission were then charged: "to enquire into the state, sufficiency and condition of the Fortifications existing for the Defence of Our United Kingdom....", to suggest improvements, to give consideration "to the most efficient means of rendering the same complete, especially all such Works of Defence as are provided for the protection of our Royal Arsenals and Dockyards...".

It was an enormous brief. The task took the Commission until February 7, 1860 when they produced their report.

The report itself is 160 pages long and its recommendations included the construction of a ring of forts to protect Plymouth on the landward side. One particular recommendation was to change the whole of Bovisand. It read: **"To ensure the security of the Sound as an anchorage for our own ships and against its occupation by an enemy, and to prevent the bombardment of the Dockyard at a long range, additional betteries to be constructed at: Picklecombe, Staddon Point, Breakwater, Hooe Lake Point, Drake's Island, Whitesand Bay, Knattenbury Hill"**.

The 1859 Commission also reported that the Staddon Height Battery was well sited, "but the works themselves are of insufficient extent, and from their construction are entirely unfit to resist the concentrated horizontal fire that could be brought to bear on them from large ships of war".

They said the same about the existing battery on Picklecombe Point. That was to undergo the same rebuilding as the Commission's report would bring to Bovisand. Picklecombe Fort is the one you can see across the Sound from Bovisand and was converted into flats in the early 1970s..

If the Commission's suggestions were all carried out, the costs would be £11,850,000. The costs of the improved defences of Plymouth would be £3,020,000, £755,000 of which was for the purchase of land and £1,915,000 for construction. The purchase of land in the case of Bovisand was not necessary. The Admiralty owned it and had done so since it was needed for building the reservoir and the watering pipeline down to the wharf at Bovisand.

On Page 34 of the report, paragraph 94 details the reasons for the extra building: **"The works that have been enumerated, will suffice to prevent the enemy from occupying the anchorage inside the breakwater, and bombarding the dockyard from that position. This latter operation is, however, still possible, by vessels lying outside the breakwater towards its eastern end, from whence part of the naval establishments are visible.**

"The fort on Staddon Point would keep small vessels from approaching the dockyard nearer than 6,500 yards; and when it is considered that the sea is seldom sufficiently smooth in this locality to afford great accuracy of practice at that range, a very destructive bombardment need not be calculated upon; although large ships might do considerable injury from that position, by throwing shells from their upper deck with rifled guns.

"But another contingency has to be provided against. The defences above mentioned may effectually preclude the enemy from occupying the Sound as an anchorage, but they do not afford a

secure refuge to ships seeking protection from a superior force, more especially at night. The forts on either side of the Sound are nearly 4,000 yards distant from each other and could not effectually support our ships inside the breakwater in the event of a sudden attack.

"We are therefore of the opinion that a powerful casemated work, of such form as to bring fire in every direction, more especially to seaward, should be constructed immediately behind the breakwater, near its centre; co-operating with the forts on each side of the Sound, and commanding the approach to both entrances from seaward".

Even while the Commission were sitting, the "rifled ordnance", which was one of the main reasons for setting up the Commission in the first place, was going into service with both the Army and the Navy. The weapon chosen was Sir William Armstrong's rifled breech-loader, the first gun to fire a cylindrical shell with a pointed nose. Six pounders, 20 and 40 pounders were introduced into both forts and ships, but were not a great success and rifled muzzle-loaders were more favoured. In 1863, Sir William Palliser invented a method of lining smooth-bore guns with a wrought-iron rifled tube and many old muzzle-loaders were converted in this way. Breech-loading didn't really win the day until 1885. The guns of Bovisand were to change over the years in a complete reflection of this battle between breech and muzzle.

Staddon Height Battery had been supported when originally built by two open battery positions - Brownhill to the North-West and Frobisher to the East. Under the new plans these two were to be abandoned. The new Staddon Point Battery (Fort Bovisand) was to be responsible together with Picklecombe and the new Breakwater Fort for blanketing the Sound with fire and destroying any enemy ships trying to enter.

Both Bovisand and Picklecombe were to be casemated works with guns mounted in rooms in the thickness of the walls and firing out through special ports. Bovisand was to have 32 guns served by 180 men. Picklecombe would mount 40 guns supported by a garrison of 200 men. And the Breakwater Fort was to be fitted with 100 guns and no less than 600 men!

Well, that is what the Commission recommended, but there wasn't that amount of money available and their suggestions were drastically pruned before any building started. However, the work did start at Bovisand and Picklecombe.

At Bovisand the first granite blocks were set in position on May 14, 1861, as authorised by a War Office letter of April 30 that year. This speed made it clear that the constructors, George Baker and Son, were not going to hang about for anyone else to change their mind. The authorised building was estimated to cost £60,000.

Bovisand was to be built of granite, though many of the other forts in the area were to use dressed limestone or other local stone. Some used a lot of slate, but not Bovisand. It was granite, granite all the way for the exterior walls of the casemates and the battery walls. The supporting arches and piers at the rear of the casemates, which you can still see today, were constructed of "well-burnt bricks, bedded and pointed in cement and sand and the whole of the roofs in concrete with asphalt finish".

The total area of Fort Bovisand when finished was to be 44,679 square feet. The plans provided for 23 casemates with magazines below for powder and shot connected to the guns above by shaft lifts. It was noted that the reason for putting the guns into casemates was "in order to protect them from fragments of shells bursting against the hill which is immediately behind the work".

Two spiral stone stair-wells were to be provided from No.6 and No.17 casemates and there was to be a main entry to the magazines at the eastern end. Trolley ways and lighting passages under the casemates were also to be built.

Because of the slope of the ground and the fact that the casemates were to follow roughly the shape of Staddon Point itself, they were to be built in a block curving through a chord of 135 degrees with the western casemates and magazines at a lower level than those to the east where the hill is steeper. In fact each one is set some inches higher than its neighbour. The lowest is 28ft 6ins and the highest 61ft 6ins above high water. This curve meant that the guns could cover most of the Sound with the main firepower aiming to the South-West. To the rear of the casemates there was to be a service road with battery offices, mess-hall and latrine building on the North side.

The old Staddon Height Battery - the top bastion of the old fort - was to be left intact and this provided barracks for the casemate gunners. The fact that the new places for the guns were to be right down almost at sea-level tells you something of the increased power of the guns then available. It was no longer necessary to try and gain extra range by building high up on a hillside.

Messrs. George Baker and Son pushed on hard with the work. And it was hard work. The granite had to come from Dartmoor, and other stone from the Breakwater quarries at Oreston. Some came by cart, but much by sea in the Breakwater barges which were still being used to dump concrete blocks on the Breakwater to repair any storm damage.

On November 25, 1869, Fort Bovisand was complete. The final cost was exactly £58,219.

Though Bovisand and the other forts resulting from the report of the 1859 Royal Commission are often called "Palmerston's Follies", they are then misnamed. Palmerston merely set up a Royal Commission in response to the public panic about a French invasion. He died in 1865 before many of the so-called "Follies" were completed.

The Guns of Bovisand.

THE fact that building Bovisand took nearly a decade seems to have been due to dithering about the kind of guns to be fitted. One set of plans visualised two tiers of casemates carrying 50 guns of 68-pounders on top of 110-pounders. The magazine for all these was drawn in as being at the rear and completely detached from the casemates. However, the case for the heavier guns with magazines underneath finally won the day.

The iron shields used in Bovisand's casemates were the latest thing in protection. New shields were tested to destruction at the Gunnery Establishment at Shoeburyness using ten-inch guns at 600 and 1,000 yards. The results showed that after 33 direct hits the casemate would probably have become untenable. After 54 hits, the gun would have been silenced. And after 86 hits, of which 22 were on the iron itself, the masonry front was destroyed, but the shields still offered a fair amount of protection.

As a result Bovisand and all the other important sea forts got the new iron armour, which afforded protection against fire at least equal to that of its own gun. The plans of Bovisand had to be modified to take these new shields. And then questions arose over the guns themselves.

In 1872, the Committee on Traversing Gear - there seemed to be a committee for everything! - came to Bovisand to watch a trial of a new type of such gear fitted to one of the Fort's 9-inch guns. Their report carefully noted that the armament at Bovisand then was 22 9-inch 12-ton guns and one 10-inch 18-ton rifled muzzle-loader.

Yet the Fort Record Book for Bovisand, which is held at the Public Record Office at Kew, and records details of the Fort year by year since its building, clearly states that the original armament of Fort Bovisand was 14 10-inch and nine 9-inch R.M.L guns. Well, at least they all agree there were 23 big guns at the Fort! In fact there were 24, because all records also agree that there was a single 7-inch 7-ton Moncrieff Disappearing Mounting gun somewhere at the Fort in 1872. Two test shots from it are reported as being fired in 1873. After that, like its name, it disappeared. We know that a special pit was dug for it in 1871, when a small training battery for new gunners was mounted somewhere on the seaward side of the present road near the speed-calming humps in the road by the Coastguard Cottages. There are traces of such a pit there and this is likely to have been the site.

What is certain is that by 1880, the 14 10-inch guns and the nine 9-inch guns were in position, all muzzle-loaders, all with rifled barrels. And in 1885, the armament was 13 10-inch guns and nine 9-inch guns, all R.M.Ls. Each gun cost nearly £4,000.

The fact that they were muzzle-loaders points up the importance of the iron shields in the casemates. Protection was vital to the gunners when reloading at the business end. And this was the reason for a while of the popularity of the Moncrieff Disappearing

This gun is using the Moncrieff Disappearing Mounting. For firing the gun is brought up to the top of the pit. Then the recoil force brings it down again for reloading under cover.

Mounting.

The strength of the recoil on these guns used a clever system of gears and counterweights to force the gun back and down, so that reloading could be done inside the shelter of the gun pit. It was then moved back up to fire over the edge of the pit once again.

Having guns that could fire out over the Sound at enemy ships was all very well, but it wasn't much use if the guns could not be locked on to one of the new steam-driven fast-moving warships. So Fort Bovisand became one of the first of the coastal defence batteries to benefit from the brains of Captain H.S.Watkin of the Royal Artillery, who, while stationed in Gibraltar, worked on this problem. He solved it with the Watkin Depression Range Finder and Position Finder. His range-finder when laid on the bow waterline of the enemy ship recorded the range and the bearing. This information was transmitted by electricity directly to the guns and, in theory anyway, the enemy ship was as good as sunk. Bovisand's accuracy was never tested in action. But it would be wrong to call Bovisand "a cushy number". The guns were always being changed and gunnery drills amended to cope with adaptations. There were and always had been plenty of practice shoots as divers know full well from the number of shot which they find anywhere to the north of the Breakwater.

The biggest upheaval came in 1896 when the 9-inch

Though this cannon is in the open air, it shows a gunner and his 10-inch RML which is one of the types of guns used in Bovisand casemates. This old picture was taken on the Isle of Wight.

When they were finished with old cannon they often just buried them. These did not come from Bovisand but are very similar. They were uncovered on Drake's Island in 1978. One of them was restored by Austin C. Carpenter, the cannon expert, (seated) and test fired by the Lord Mayor of Plymouth.

guns were removed from the casemates. They had become outdated. Oddly enough, this meant a retreat up the hill to the upper level of the old fort, where the original guns had been set to increase their range. This latest move was nothing to do with getting extra distance on the shot, but so that the new guns could fire over the casemates.

By authority of the War Office, Devonport, on June 14, 1898, work was put in hand to build emplacements for a 12-pounder quick-firing battery on the lower level of the old fort of 1845 with a field of fire over the casemates, which had been completed just 25 years before. The new battery was to be four quick-firing 12-pounder 12cwt. guns.

The intention was still to defend Plymouth Sound, but this time the specification, estimated cost £2,500, was to include a large number of "Defence Electric Light Positions". Today we would call these searchlights, but in those days the artilleryman would call them by their initials, D.E.Ls. The installation of "Dells" really showed the way things in the world of war were changing. Later the lights were called "C.A.S.Ls" (Coastal Artillery Search Lights), but the idea was the same - to light up any fast enemy boats rushing in to the Sound to create havoc among the naval forces and friendly shipping anchored there.

The guns of Bovisand's casemates were removed in order as they were judged obsolete - in 1896 the 9-inch guns went, in 1903 four of the 10-inch were removed and six more the following year. In 1905, the last four were withdrawn.

But before the final removal, a battery of four quick-firing 12-pounders were already in position. On completion date - November 15, 1898 - the work had cost less than the estimate of £2,500. The War Office must have been pleased with the real bill of £1,890.

Today we know a great deal about how the Fort looked at the beginning of the century and how it operated. The reason for this knowledge is that a Lance Corporal W. Hayes of the Royal Engineers, who was stationed at Fort Bovisand in 1900, was detailed off to make a comprehensive plan of the Fort and the battery. He finished his work on June 17, 1901 and his drawings are still in the Public Record Office today.

Corporal Hayes did his work well. On his plan (scale 10 feet to an inch), we can see where the guns

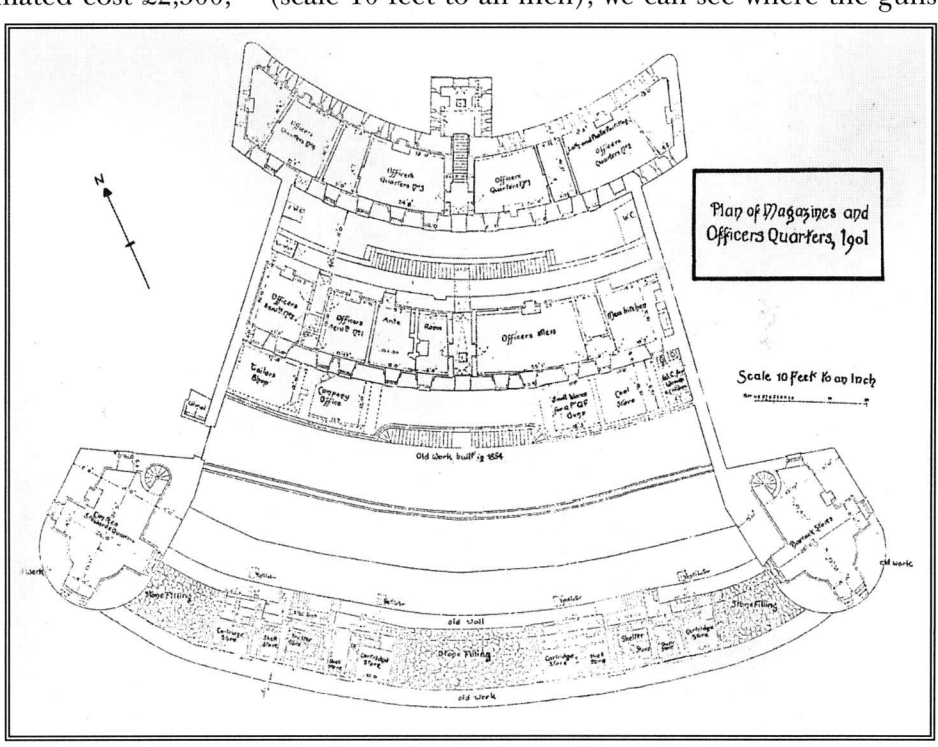

This is part of the plan that Hayes drew of the fort as he saw it in 1901.

were sited, where the shell store was underneath each gun position, where the cartridge stores were... in fact absolutely everything about the operation of that battery. We even know where counter was in the canteen in the stump of the West Tower. That the similar stump of East Tower housed the company stores. Both towers had been trimmed right down during the work of 1898 to allow the guns up there a full field of fire.

Thanks to Corporal Hayes, we know where the officers lived, where their mess was, where their batmen lived, where the tailor's ship was, where the coal was kept - vital information if you had to live in those cold great stone buildings in the winter!

The plan showed where the drawbridge was at the top level leading across the defensive dry ditch at the top of the old Fort. That in turn explains the rifle slits in the wall of the private flat there!

Once their guns had gone, what happened to the casemates? There was no thought of knocking them down. They had been built to last forever and even today seem likely to do so. They suffered from damp, particularly in the underground magazines area, but they were still used. By 1901, a battery of six Hotchkiss quick-firing 6-pounder 8cwt guns were mounted in pairs on the top of the casemates to add to the Fort's

This aerial of the Staddon Height Battery shows where the two flanking towers were on that top fortification.

firepower out over the Sound. Automatic sights were added to them in February, 1903. And we also know from Corporal Hayes's careful work that they had a separate ammunition store, above ground and not in the casemates themselves. At the same time two Maxim guns were erected on the stumps of each of the two towers (cut down to first storey level) of the old Fort up the hillside. The magazines of the casemates were also used to house the power units for the "Dells" to enable their beams to criss-cross over the surface of the Sound.

The armament of Fort Bovisand was now settled for the next 44 years! That is the length of time from their installation in 1898 that the 12-pounder 12cwt. guns were to be the main armament of the Fort. They lasted in fact until January 1942.

Kill the Queen Bee!

BEFORE consigning the casemates to their gunless years, it is interesting to note that the War Office and the Navy of those years were not as dim as they were often painted, or cartooned. They had, in fact, correctly assessed the threat of the speed which steam engines had given to ships and from as early as 1869, when the Whitehead torpedo first appeared in England, they directed their guns and gunnery to the problem of dealing with fast steam ships, eqipped with such missiles.

The world's first real torpedoboat was H.M.S. Lightning, launched in 1876 and modified three years later to carry two Whitehead torpedoes in above water tubes. The success of Lightning made sure that other navies promptly followed suit. Steam turbines were soon to make ships even faster.

The Royal Navy thought of ports like Plymouth, shuddered and set the coastal defence forts to work. Live ammunition practices became the order of the day rather than dummy drills. These practices were designed to ensure that enemy torpedo boats could be wiped out before they could enter the Sound and sink Britain's great warships at anchor there.

Simulating such an attack was a problem. The practices themselves were called "Hong Kongs". This odd name came from the targets, which the Navy called that for some reason that remains obscure. They were towed by a launch at the end of a very long rope. Winches on the towing ship could haul in the target at high speed. This simulated the dash of a torpedoboat or even a destroyer. When live ammunition was used, the captain of the towing vessel often abandoned the target as the shellspouts all around him made it clear that he was dealing with a bunch of new recruits to the world of coastal gunnery!

Gunners were used to regular practices.

The skippers of the towing launches regularly tried to claim danger money and their language on their return to the harbour at Bovisand after some particularly near-miss was much admired by all the gunners, who had reached a high peak in the use of foul language during their time servicing the guns in the casemates.

The life of a gunner in the Bovisand casemates was not a happy one. In the back of his mind the whole time was the knowledge that the neat and obvious row of casemates would certainly be a prime target of any wartime attack. Secondly, he knew that though he was protected by the iron shield, this would not last long against the latest shells from rifled guns with their greater penetrating power.

Then, to add to his woes, the firing of the guns resulted in clouds of acrid smoke. After the first few rounds, the ventilation system usually failed to work and he worked on in a thick evil-smelling fog. He longed for a transfer to another unit, which had the good fortune of operating guns in the open. All works after 1880 had the guns mounted in the open air.

The live-ammo practices continued at Bovisand despite the gunners' discomfort. Much to the delight of the skippers of the target-towing launches, a new kind of boat was used for later practices. These new boats were small, but radio-controlled and the Navy called them either Queen Bees or Queen Gulls. The Queen Bee was the smaller of the two types.

One of these boats, a Queen Gull, was stored in a shed at the landward end of Bovisand harbour, near today's launching ramp.

Each of the big guns in the casemates had its own detachment, under the command of a Gun Captain, a non-commissioned officer, who had permanent charge of the gun, was responsible for its condition and cleanliness, all the stores connected with it, and for the state of the casemate itself.

Next in line of command was the Gun Layer, who actually aimed the gun, seeing that it was correctly traversed on to the target. This was checked by means of a pointer against the arc let into the floor of the casemate (parts of these arcs can be seen in a very few of the casemates today; the vandals took them for the brass).

Seven more men made up the rest of the gun detachment. They were numbered from No.2 to No.8. Each had a special job to do.

No.2 had to insert the gas check to the projectile. The gas check was to prevent the gas escaping round the shell when the gun was fired, but it also had projections which fitted into the rifling and gave the shot the necessary spin. In addition the No.2. was responsible for hooking and unhooking the hoisting tackle, he had to steady and guide the projectile into the muzzle, ram it home, close the mantlet, help with swivelling or traversing the gun, and look after some of the sponges.

The "mantlet" needs explaining. If you look in some of the casemates at Bovisand, you will see things like giant curtain rods inside the iron shields of the casemates. They were a kind of curtain rod, but from the rod and rings hung two "mantlets", curtains of woven rope, which were pulled from each side around the chase (front portion) of the gun in action. The idea was to prevent the enemy's return fire from sending stone fragments chipped off the outer stone bouncing round inside the casemate. They were tested and issued to Bovisand in 1872. They also helped to keep smoke from the muzzle out of the casemate, but had to be continually soaked with water to prevent them catching fire from the muzzle flashes.

No.3 was a gun loader. He shifted the hoisting tackle, steadied and guided the projectile, uncapped the fuse or removed the safety pin, closed the mantlet, traversed and looked after sponges.

No.4 supplied sidearms to the gun crew in case of an assault by ground troops, rammed home, elevated, fired and opened one side of mantlet.

No.5 attended to the snatch block and lower block of

hoisting tackle, raised the projectile, rammed home, supplied wedge wads, elevated and opened mantlet on his side.

No.6 attended to cartridge lift and supplied cartridges to No.3, removed empties.

No.7. attended to shell lift, fixed fuses, brought up and raised projectiles and removed empties.

No.8. assisted No.7 at the shell lift and brought up and raised projectiles.

Each man had a full load of work during firing and the drills were practised day after dreary day. But with 12 tons of gun hurtling about on the recoil, there was no time or room for mistakes or day-dreaming. Accidents were frequent. A moment's inattention during firing could mean a crushing injury or death.

The gun was everything. The gun crew lived in the casemate with it at the seaward end. And there was no sloppiness in their quarters. "Bull" and "spit and polish" were the rule. The gun had to be ready at all times. The manual laid it all down: "The bores of the guns when not in use will be lacquered; when practice is being carried out they will be kept slightly oiled, to prevent rusting. At the close of each day's practice they will accordingly be washed out. As soon as dry they will be oiled with a greasy sponge and the muzzles closed with tampeons". And that was only the bores. There was a whole long list of daily maintenance for each part of the gun and its stores as well.

In that same manual for the Mark VI 9-inch R.M.L, it is carefully noted that the maximum range for that gun was 10,230 yards. At that distance the projectile was in flight for 45.5 seconds. During the shell's flight drift of 300 yards had to be allowed for (no wonder the target-towers complained!). Muzzle velocity was 1194 f.s. And to get all that you loaded a charge of 50lbs of powder and a Palliser projectile of 360lbs.

The gunner's life was indeed a dreary one, all practice and no action. This was acknowledged by the building of married quarters in 1912. They were built close to the existing coastguard station and today you pass them on the way down to the Fort. The coastguard station was originally built of shellit, and was designed to have front and side walls of hung slates. In 1940, it was still lit by oil lamps!

Breakwater Fort Ahead.

THOUGH the Royal Commission of 1859 had specified that a four-storey granite fort should be built just behind the centre of the Breakwater, it ended up being mostly made of iron.

The idea of a Fort in the centre of the Sound was not new. The Duke of Wellington had suggested it in 1820. He said that such a fort would protect the whole of the Sound against enemy shipping. An estimate then put the cost of a fort at the Breakwater at £43,000. Those against the Duke's plan said that such a fort could do no more that a few ships anchored behind the Breakwater could do. The antis won the day and the idea was dropped. Of course, it surfaced again in the 1859 report together with the recommendation that it should be placed near the Shovel Rock at the centre of the Breakwater.

The original plan of the Commission for this fort to hold 100 guns and 600 men was clearly ridiculous. There wasn't the money. Nor the guns. Nor the men. But there was the need for a fort.

During their work the Commission had discovered that the guns on either side of the Sound - at Maker and at Staddon Heights - could not completely close the Sound to enemy shipping and there were significant gaps in the curtain of fire that those forts could lay down. So they said:"A powerful casemated work of such a form as to bring fire to bear in every direction, more especially to seaward, should be constructed immediately behind the Breakwater and near to its centre". A small stump of the Shovel Rock still emerged from under the Breakwater and work began using that as the fort's foundation.

The original plan for the Breakwater Fort was for four storeys of granite work with 40 guns behind iron shields in casemates. The foundations went down, but then there was a hold-up. The Shoeburyness Gunnery Establishment were carrying out tests on iron and its resistance to modern gunfire. They did the same with granite structures. The results, said those experts at Shoeburyness, proved that a structure of iron was more likely to stand up to heavy enemy fire than one of stone.

So the plan for the Breakwater Fort changed again. The new scheme was for a two-storey iron fort with 18 guns on the top and the magazines underneath. And that is basically what you see when you look out from Bovisand to the Breakwater today.

Plymouth Ocean Projects, which is the company which holds the lease of Fort Bovisand from the M.O.D., also has a licence on the Breakwater Fort, which is mostly used for training commercial divers. You might think, looking at it from a distance, that the Breakwater Fort is all stone, but get closer and you can see just how much iron has been used. The area which housed the guns is all iron.

This fort is 144 feet long and 114 feet wide. It stands 105 yards behind the Breakwater itself and is 1,400 yards from Bovisand's casemates. The foundations which were sunk before the change of plans, are 10m below mean sea level and were put in

The Breakwater Fort. It was originally designed to have four storeys and 40 guns.

place by divers working from a square-shaped bell. A nice thought for those on commercial courses as they work on the seabed below the Breakwater Fort today.

Work was begun on the Breakwater Fort in 1867, but was halted while the new design underwent more gunnery trials at Shoeburyness. You could hardly call those tests superficial - a 12-inch 25-ton R.M.L., a 10-inch 18-ton R.M.L. and a 15-inch American Rodman R.M.L. were all set up just 200 yards from the ironwork. They fired 37 rounds at it. Even after that the experts said it was still "defensible" even if somewhat second-hand! So the work on the Breakwater Fort went ahead once more. It was finished in 1870. In 1880, the fort's armament was fourteen 12.5 inch and four 10-inch rifled muzzle-loaders. Now it needed the "eyes" of a Watkin Rangefinder and this was installed as soon as the one at Bovisand became operational. Information to the guns of the Breakwater Fort were fed by submarine cable from finders on the old fort at Bovisand and Fort Picklecombe.

The guns of the Breakwater Fort became obsolete at the same time as those of Bovisand and Picklecombe and after they were removed the rest of its Service life was as a Naval signal station. The signal station of modern times was built on its roof.

War To End All Wars.

BOVISAND, together with the rest of Britain, drowsed into the hot Summer of 1914. The garrison of the Fort were rudely awoken in August when the world went to war. The number of men at the Fort trebled in as many weeks. Gun drills became more frequent now they had a real enemy in mind, but they still centred on the main armament of those four quick-firing 12-pounder guns, which dated back to 1898.

But enemy came there none. It seemed that even the Zeppelins had no designs on Bovisand. All the action was elsewhere.

Plymouth itself was a centre for supplying the fodder for such action - men, guns and ammunition. As a garrison town and a great Naval port, Plymouth was the hub of a great swirl of activity. Thousands of men, many former Territorials, trained in the camps round about. They in turn became infantry, forming county regiments, the Devons and the Duke of Cornwall's, for example, before streaming aboard ships headed for every theatre of war.

At the same time as these home-grown troops left for the battlefields, other troops poured into Plymouth Docks, many from the Dominions and India. The First Canadian Expeditionary Force, for example, sailed in past Bovisand after crossing the Atlantic in flotilla of 30 liners and disembarked with all its own guns, horses and munitions at the Dockyard.

Bovisand was put on alert for submarines. In fact, the area around Plymouth went spy crazy with tales of men with German accents rowing ashore with radio sets from German U-boats. The threat to the Dockyards from the U-boats themselves was, however, taken more seriously. Booms were spread out across the Sound entrances and one, sealing the Eastern Channel, had its shore end at Bovisand (a similar boom was put in place during World War Two).

Most nights there were alarms. Eye-witnesses say that then the Sound became fairyland. "Dells" beamed out across the waters literally turning night into day. "The waters shone like burnished silver," said one particularly poetic onlooker. But the light never fell on a U-boat's conning-tower, even when the sinking of merchantmen only a short way off the coast proved that the young German commanders were bringing their U-boats down the Channel on a regular basis.

The German submarine menace was real enough. More and more ships were sunk off the Devon and Cornish coast and by the end of the war, nearly 800 Allied ships had been sunk in the Channel by U-boats with torpedoes, mines or gunfire. That number of ships sunk is not surprising when you remember that the Channel, already the busiest shipping lane in the world, was crammed with more ships than ever during the four years of war.

The First World War with its vast expenditure of men and munitions in the trenches of France created a huge demand. And everything that Britain needed to carry on that war had to come by sea. Britain relied on shipping too for much of its food so it was only commonsense for Germay to try and cut those lifelines.

Their weapon was the U-boat. And most of the submarines which preyed around Plymouth came from the Flanders Flotilla, whose boats were based in Bruges after the German Army over-ran the Belgian ports such as Zeebrugge, which gave access to the canals connecting Bruges to the sea.

Those Unterwasserbooten had to run the gauntlet of the mines and nets of the Dover Barrage before coming down the Channel to Devon and Cornwall. There were three main types of U-boat. The U-class started the war as small boats, but grew in size as the war went on. They had both bow and stern torpedo tubes and a speed of 15 knots on the surface, 5 knots submerged. Then there was the UB-class. These were slower (13 knots; 4 knots submerged), but carried an 88mm gun on the deck. And finally, the UC-class were minelayers, capable of laying a field of 18 mines from special chutes, but also carrying torpedoes and a deck gun. All had an operating range of thousands of miles and so considered a run down to Plymouth a mere doddle. Some of the victims of those missions to the South-West are detailed in the diving sections which follow later in this book.

The Royal Navy meanwhile were running a blockade of their own. So effective was it that most of the German civilian population lived under near starvation conditions. That national hunger is said to be the main reason for the Kaiser launching the German U-boats into "unrestricted" campaign of February 1,1917. This basically meant that the submarines could sink any ship on sight in the Channel and most other sea areas.

This new U-boat offensive was disastrous for Britain and the U-boats sank so much shipping that at one time there was only enough food in Britain to feed the nation for three weeks. Only the introduction of convoys, the entry of the United States into the war, and the complete closing of the Straits of Dover with mines and nets, plus the creation of the Northern barrage of mines from the Orkneys to Norway, turned the war around.

Plymouth paid a big part in the defeat of the U-boats, not only providing a base and servicing for the Royal Navy's submarine-hunters of all types, but in fitting out the Q-ships, which pretended to be a simple merchantmen - until a U-boat surfaced nearby. Then screens dropped down to reveal big guns. Navy gunners then used those guns to pour shells into the attacker from short range.

Towards the end of the war, the convoy system began cutting dramatically the losses caused by U-boats. During one short period 138 convoys made up of 6,000,000 tons of shipping were guarded in and out of Plymouth by the Royal Navy with losses of less than six per cent.

However, Plymouth families suffered huge casualties in naval battles, and in the merciless trench warfare in France. At Jutland, for example, five of the lost ships were mostly manned by former reservists from Devonport. Plymouth casualties from that battle neared the thousand mark.

Work in the Dockyard boomed, doubling the workforce from 10,000 men to 20,000. They built the 25,750-ton battleship Royal Oak and the 3,750-ton lightcruiser Cleopatra, and two of the K-class submarines.

If things were quiet at Bovisand, the war certainly came to Plymouth. Turnchapel in the Cattewater, where the Admiralty had bought the wharves and the quarries behind for oil storage in 1905, became almost a submarine base with queues of the slim black boats waiting to refuel.

The Americans, when they joined the war in 1917, made their base at Victoria Wharves, which were soon packed with destroyers and submarine-chasers. At Mount Batten the Royal Naval Air Service set up their base using blimps, balloons and the first of the Short seaplanes. At first these had to be lifted in and out of the water by cranes. Later slipways were built.

When the war was over, Bovisand sank deep into peace. The gun practices went on, but Bovisand Bay became a favourite resort of picknickers, who came not only by road, but by boats from Plymouth itself. A guide of the time describes Bovisand like this:" There are good sands and several quiet bays with facilities for bathing, while light refreshments may be obtained in the tea huts and cottages". The flood of Plymothians to Bovisand with caravans and beach chalets was still in the future, though during the summer holidays plenty of tents sprouted in the valley.

But there were changes. Even though the general rule that after a war everything goes to pot, applied as usual to Bovisand and the area roundabout, the rundown was fairly gentle.

The gunners kept the Fort going, but the big garrison of the 1914-18 war dwindled away. The local Territorials wisely stayed enthusiastic and trained on the remaining four quick-firing 12-pounders, which had done nearly 40 years service as the first whisps of new storm clouds gathered over Europe.

Mount Batten became the home of two flying boat squadrons of the R.A.F. and the garrison at Bovisand became very used to seeing those great ships of the air, the Sunderlands, landing and taking off in the Sound. A certain Aircraftsman Shaw served there as the station-commander's runner. Shaw witnessed and was involved in three fatal air crashes into the Sound and his experiences led him into campaigning within the R.A.F. for a high-speed air-sea rescue launch service. His campaigning was highly effective - Aircraftsman Shaw was better known as Lawrence of Arabia!

There were changes at Fort Bovisand. Casemates were put to many different uses, but the basic layout was as follows: Casemate 1 and 2 were engine rooms to provide lighting. Originally, these engines were Hornby horizontals. In 1928, they were changed to Crossley petrol engines (in 1940, they were to change again to four Dorman 22kw and a Lister 12kw).

Casemate 3 was the accumulator room and Casemate 4 was the N.C.Os canteen with the other ranks canteen in No.5. Casemate 6 was the library. No.7 was accommodation for 9 men, while No.8 held ten. Numbers 9,10 and 11 were company offices.

Casemates 12,13 and 14 were more sleeping accommodation. No.15 and No.16 held the sergeants' mess and kitchen. From No.17 to No.22 were men's quarters. Casemate No.23 was the Cookhouse. In all, this provided for one warrant officer, six staff sergeants and sergeants, and 127 corporals, lance-corporals and privates. Nine married soldiers were in the married quarters and four officers lived in the old fort up the hill.

The buildings behind casemates 7-11 were used as the artillery store and fitters shop, while the buildings behind casemates 15,16 and17 were the blacksmith's shop and paint stores. The coal supply was stored down by the front gate in the end of the casemate block. The men's latrines were down there too, exactly where they are today. On the left side of the main gate as you faced it was the guard room. On the quay of the little port were four small derricks and a crane.

Bovisand Hits Back.

HITLER marched. And on August 24,1939, the Territorial Army was mobilised. The Devon Heavy Regiment R.A. (T.A.) and the Devon and Cornwall (Fortress) Royal Engineers were among them. The Artillery mustered at Lambhay Hill, Plymouth, and the Royal Engineers at Mutley Barracks.

They called those four old faithful guns at the Fort the Bovisand Battery and 157 Battery Royal Artillery were ordered to take charge of them and to man the Fort together with No.3 Company of the Devon and Cornwall (Fortress) R.E.s. The first lorry with the first of those men drew up outside the main gate at 5 a.m. on August 25. In command of 157 Battery was Lieutenant T.K.Hitchins with 2nd Lieutenants J.W.Best and E.L.Endicott as section commanders. The R.E.Company was commanded by 2nd Lieutenant Pannall. Preparing the guns for action started at once. "Battery ready" was reported to the Fire Commander at 0800hrs.

At 1600hrs that same date, the second watch took over and 400 shells filled with Lyddite were fused and 100 allocated to each gun.

The first manning strength return was made on August 29: Royal Artillery. Officers 3; Other ranks 63; Attached 5.
Royal Engineers. Officers 1; Other ranks 44. On August 30, the Fort was inspected by Lieut-Colonel J.G.M.B.Cooke of the Royal Artillery, who was in command of the Devon Heavy Regiment.

On September 3,1939, the war game became a real one. Within a few moments of Chamberlain broadcasting to the nation that we were at war with Germany, the air raid sirens wailed for the first time over Plymouth and the Sound. At Bovisand, the guns were manned, but the steady high note of the all-clear soon followed. However, the war was very, very soon to become all too real for the people of Plymouth.

The 22,500-ton aircraft-carrier Courageous, crewed almost entirely by Devon sailors, most of them from Plymouth, sailed out of the Sound on a Saturday a few days later. Lieutenant Hitchins, who was standing by

Lieutenant T.K. Hitchins (third from left, back row) and some of the off-duty members of 157 Battery Royal Artillery, who manned Bovisand from the beginning of World War Two.

The last photograph ever taken of H.M.S Courageous. She is shown leaving Plymouth Sound in September 1939. The next day she was sunk.

the casemates taking photographs for the records, saw her go and almost automatically raised his camera and took her picture. It was to be the last photograph ever taken of her. The next day, Sunday, the 17th of September, 1939, she was torpedoed by U-29 commanded by Kapitan-leutnant Otto Schuhart at 2020hrs. Courageous sank swiftly with the loss of 578 men.

The work of getting the Fort up to full operation went on at speed. In 1939, there were four Coastal Artillery Searchlights (C.A.S.L.s) in emplacements at the Fort. Two were on the road leading down to the Fort and two fixed-beams were in a double emplacement near the base of Bovisand pier on the seaward side of the road outside Casemates 4 and 5. Two more lights were added in 1940 when the Royal Artillery relieved the Fortress Company of the Royal Engineers of their searchlight duties. Certain R.E.s remained at the Fort for engine room work until 1942.

In those early years the guns remnained the same 12-pounders. It sounds incredible that these old guns should still be the fort's main armament. But it isn't when you know that at the outbreak of the 1939 war, the whole of England and Wales were defended by only 139 guns in all! And of those, 31 were the dear old 12-pounders. If the Germans had stayed behind the Maginot Line, the rearming of Britain would have gone at a very slow pace, but when France collapsed and invasion became a real threat, guns were taken from any source and set up to cover any invasion-likely spot around Britain.

Many of these guns were taken from old Royal Navy warships scrapped in the 1920s. Within a year of the start of the war, 510 Naval guns had been recovered from the scrapheaps, restored, remounted and manned. Bovisand didn't get any. After all, they had their 12-pounders!

Such a situation couldn't last. The war was going disastrously for Britain. One bright spot was the scuttling of the pocket-battleship Graf Spee and, past Bovisand, into the anchorage of the Sound came the battered, but victorious, cruisers Ajax and Exeter. On February 16, 1940, Winston Churchill visited both ships in the Dockyard at Devonport. He knew what a morale-raiser such a visit would be and so it was.

On land it was a different story, the German armies raced through France to the coast and out of Dunkirk came the shattered remnants of the British and French armies. Some 80,000 French troops were evacuated to Plymouth and then, in one of the most amazing and disastrous decisions of the war, were shipped back to France to fight on. In fact, they went almost straight into German prisoner-of-war camps when France surrendered in June,1940. Now the Luftwaffe had air-bases in France, close enough to raid the whole of Britain. The first bombs fell on Plymouth in July. But most of the Battle of Britain was fought in the skies over London and the South-East.

The real hell from the air as far as Plymouth was concerned came in 1941. On the nights of March 20 and March 21, waves of German bombers hit the docks and the city. By the time the all-clear was given there were 250 civilians dead and thousands homeless. But the German bombers came back in April. Five nights of raids starting on April 21 left the centre of the city gutted and another 750 civilians dead.

Though the guns of Bovisand were useless against the bombers, they must have caused some annoyance to the bomber crews with their searchlights. Bombs were aimed at the Fort. Two were direct hits. One landed very close to the Artificers Shop at the rear of Casemate 9 and the other directly on top of the casemates. Amazingly, both failed to explode! Which was not the case with the many near-misses in the countryside or the large quantity which fell into the sea near the Fort.

Much of fire that was directed at hit-and-run bombers during daylight hours, came from Lewis guns and Brens. One former Royal Artillery officer at Bovisand told me recently that he personally emptied many a Bren magazine at these single raiders, though he could not claim any visible result of his fire.

The German hit-and-run raiders had learned to shelter under the Sunderland flying boats as they returned from long patrols to their base at Mount Batten. No one dared fire. At the last possible minute, the German would veer away and bomb and machine gun Plymouth docks and buildings close by.

One was not clever enough. On a clear evening in 1941, the pilot either left the shelter of the Sunderland too early or got too far away for the flying-boat to give him full protection and became a clear target for the guns on Drake's Island. They opened up and the bomber was hit almost at once. He crashed into the Sound. It was still daylight and the sound of the people of Plymouth cheering could be heard almost across the whole of the Sound! It was a boost for their morale after the misery of the Blitz.

That year Bovisand was still carrying out improvements. New searchlights were installed on the rocks in front of the fort. No1 and No.2 lights were well up the road from the fort as was No.6. No.3 light was in front of Casemate 17, No.4 light in front of Casemate 20 and No.5 was opposite Casemate 23. Lights 3,4,5 and 6 were fixed beam and the old emplacement for the two fixed beams by the harbour was abandoned. More lights need more power, so the old accumulator room in Casemate 3 was turned into another engine room with three more Dorman 22kw installed.

In the event of total failure of the engines and the searchlights, emergency illumination of the Sound was to be provided by two Ryder flare equipments and these were on the rocks almost exactly in front of Casemate 12. These in turn were replaced by four Lyon searchlights of 26cm on May 27,1943.

The German E-boats (motor-torpedo boats) were much feared by those responsible for the defence of the Sound. Spotlighting any such raider was to be the task of the searchlights at the Fort. To speed up the rangefinding of a target hurtling in at 40 knots meant fitting new gear - Director Mark 13s arrived at the Fort in May and July of 1941.

But if this new equipment speeded up fire, it is extremely doubtful if those old 12-pounders could have coped with such high-speed work. There were only three of the "old faithfuls" now. One had been sent over to Fort Picklecombe.

Change when it came was more about name changing than new guns. From the First of June, 1941, the Devon Heavy Regiment ceased to exist as such. All coast artillery units were renamed Coast Regiments and Coast Batteries. Under this new grouping, 157 Heavy Battery Royal Artillery who were manning Bovisand, became 158 Coast Battery and a part of 568 Coast Regiment, Royal Artillery, which had its headquarters at Wembury.

This change must have been a bit confusing for the officers and men, but they had hardly time to adapt to their change of name before 158 Coast Battery was sent to relieve 137 Coast Battery in the Orkneys. And 137 came to Bovisand. The change of weather must have been a great relief to them!

After nearly 44 years in service, the armament of the Fort was unchanged. But the rumours began to fly among the gunners at Bovisand. Something big was about to happen. Or so someone said!

Rapid Fire!

It had been known since the start of the war that the defences of Plymouth were hopelessly out of date. In any attack on Plymouth itself, German naval forces, if they had managed to get past the Royal Navy and into range of the Sound, would have run very little risk from the defensive guns of forts like Bovisand.

It is amazing that a high-speed German force did not stage, or at least try, a "blitzkrieg "on Britain's largest naval port. The net boom, which now ran from Bovisand to the Breakwater and covered as well the Western Channel, may have kept out German submarine commanders wanting to emulate the exploits of Gunther Prien of U-47. (In 1939 he had penetrated deep into the Royal Navy stronghold of Scapa Flow and torpedoed H.M.S.Royal Oak.) Such dash and daring might have caused a similar disaster in Plymouth Sound.

That attack never came, but the mere thought of it put the needs of places like Bovisand well to the forefront. The guns of Fort Bovisand would be changed as soon as possible and they would be chosen with the thought of a "blitzkrieg" much in mind.

Two 10-ton lorries arrived at the main gate of Fort Bovisand early in 1942. The first arrived on January 29; the second two days later on January 31. On each lorry was the mounting, weighing 5.25 tons, for 6-pounder twin 10cwt guns. These twins were the reason for fitting the modern Director 13 rangefinders the previous year. Together they provided the answer to the rapid fire needed to engage the German E-boats. In fact they were known as the "Anti-MTB" gun and could pour out 70 rounds per minute from the twin barrels set in each mounting. They were to be placed in position on the top of the casemates complete with armoured shields.

Getting the mountings to Bovisand was one thing.

Two of these twin six-pounders were mounted on top of the casemates in 1942. They were intended to beat off any German E-boat attacks on shipping in the Sound.

How Bovisand intended to defend itself to the last in 1942.

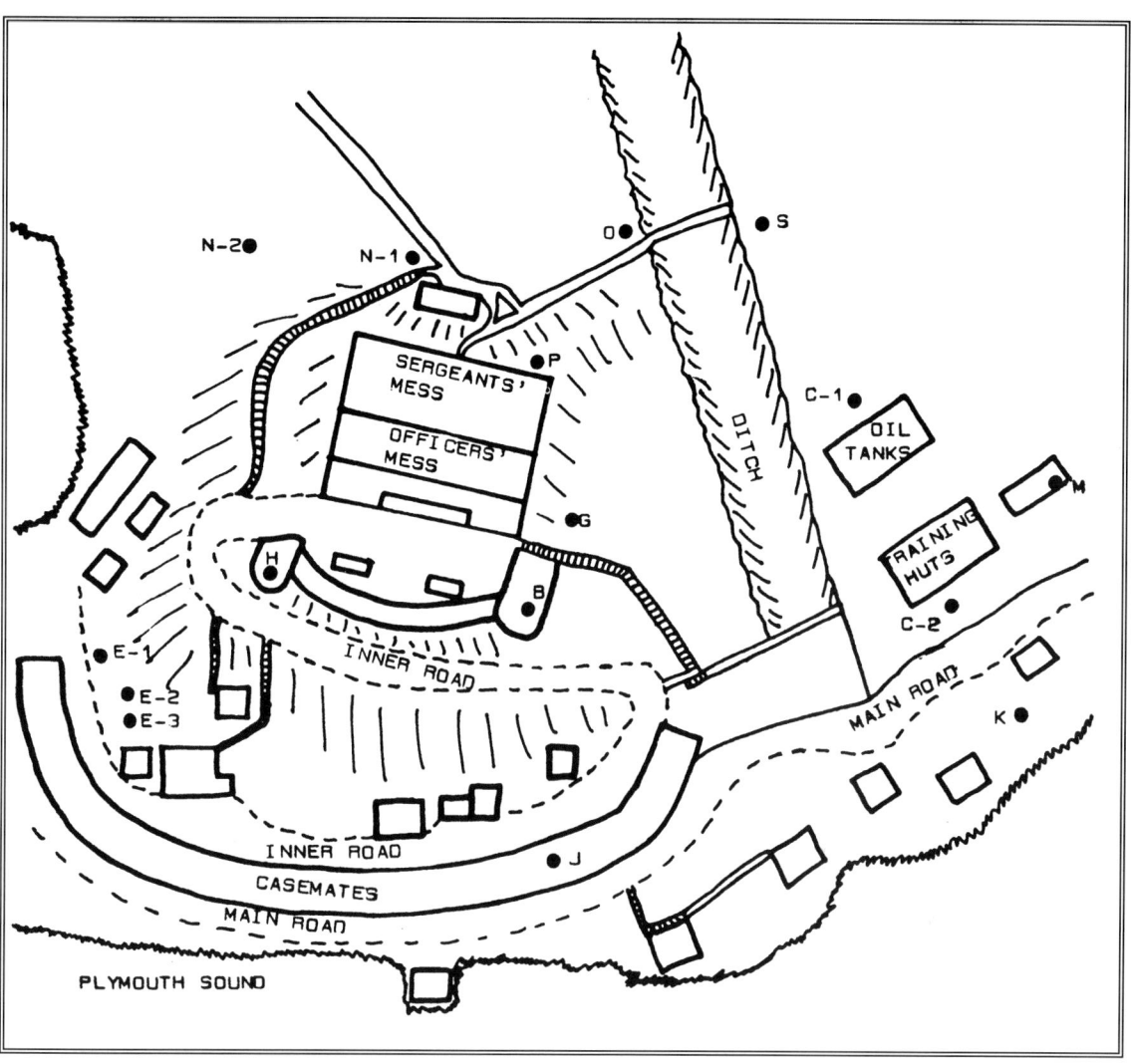

UPPER SECTOR

O   Bren, MG, Rifles, Grenades
P   Spigot Mortar
S   Rifles
N-1 Rifles, Grenades
N-2 Rifles, Grenades
H   Spigot Mortar, Bren, MG
B   Spigot Mortar
G   Rifles, Grenades

LOWER SECTOR

E-1 Rifles, Grenades
E-2 Support E-1 with Rifles
E-3 As above
J   Bren, MG, Grenades
K   Rifles, Grenades
C-1 Rifles, Grenades
C-2 Rifles, Grenades
M   Bren, MG, Grenades

Getting them up to the top of the casemates was quite another. And if the men of 137 Coast Battery looked at the task with awe, they were not allowed to goggle for long before 2nd Lieutenant G.H.Brown of the Royal Artillery got them all to work.

The problem was simply to lift all that metal over the parapet on the top of the casemates, a height of 25ft 6inches. First job was to get them off the lorries. This was done by jacks and a ramp from the lorry to the road in front of the casemates. A primitive sleigh was them built under the mounting and it was pulled into position.

No.1 gun was to go on top of Casemate 11 and No.2 on top of Casemate 16.

Second Lieutenant Brown then started the the big lift. By using a derrick, and various backstays, he could lift the mountings up, but not high enough to get them over the parapet. The solution was to raise the foot of the derrick about two feet above road level. It finally all went well, but the mountings still lacked rather important parts - the barrels! There was quite a wait for these. The barrels, or pieces as the R.A.likes to call them, arrived from Canvey Island on March 30. Each of the barrels weighed a little over 8cwt. However, much to Lieutenant Brown's obvious fury, there were only two barrels, enough for one mounting only. Twelve men hauled each of them up to the top of the casemate and the work took 16 days to complete.

But the new guns had to wait until November 28 for another barrel to arrive and then until January 8,1943 for the final one!

But what happened to the original 12-pounders? One we know was sent to Fort Picklecombe. Two more were confidently despatched to Ceylon via Millbay Docks on March 7,1942. The Fort Record Book at the time gloomily noted: "It is doubtful if these 'Old Timers' ever reached their destination, as no acknowledgement of their receipt was ever received". Well, it could be true that they never reached Ceylon - another reliable source told me that they turned up in Paignton! Certainly we know for sure that the last 12-pounder was dismantled and sent back to Central Ordnance, Donnington on May 9,1942.

But Bovisand had got some modern armaments. Her defensive capabilities were increased at the same time with the old Lewis guns being replaced in 1942 by more Brens and three spigot mortars. These, together with hand grenades and Lee Enfield .303 rifles, were their total defence against any land attack. It is clear that such an attack had not been ruled out. A defence plan made by members of the garrison at that time is reproduced on the previous page.

In 1942, another plan was drawn up. This was a layout of the Fort and shows the uses to which various parts were being put. On June 28, 1942, Second Lieutenant M.C.Hay of the Royal Artillery, who was stationed at the Fort, produced the plan.

You will note from that plan that a lighter element had come into the life of the garrison. Casemate 3 had now become a billiard room. Casemate 4 had become the Medical Room and it is amusing to note that young Hay marked a portion of that room as storage for "sports gear". Well, in the wartime Army they were called many things!

Casemate 5 was a lecture hall and the magazine to feed both the new 6-pounders was in today's Reception. The shell hoists were on either side of this casemate. Several new buildings of the Nissen-hut variety had appeared on the road. The Guard Room had now been moved from down by the Main Gate near the harbour to a position on the road by No.2 searchlight, where there was also a training hut and a reserve oil store with a capacity of 12 x 600 gallons.

It was interesting to hear from one ex-member of the R.A. stationed at Bovisand in the war that there were never, ever, any members of the women's services at Fort Bovisand. When I showed him the maps and diagrams made during the war years

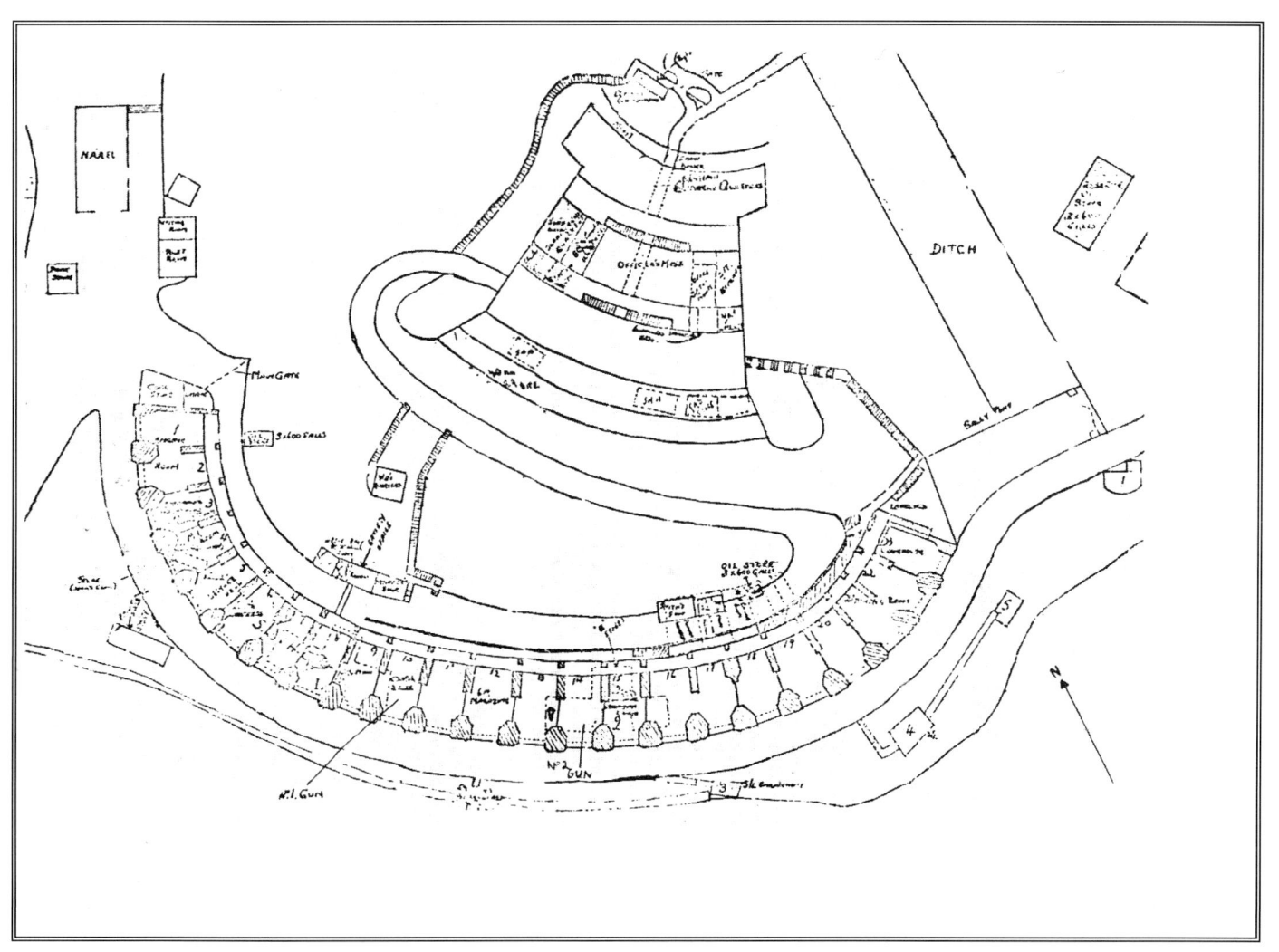

Second Lieutenant M.C.Hay of the Royal Artillery drew this plan on June 28, 1942.

showing "Wrens' Duty Room", "Wrens Welfare room", even "Wren accommodation", he brushed it all aside saying even more firmly: "Women were never at Bovisand". He should see it today! But he is wrong. Wrens were there. In small numbers, but they were there.

Another building, which does not exist today, as it was on ground now occupied by the luxury accommodation block down by the harbour, was the NAAFI, which, I suspect was no different from any other wartime Naafi in the quality of the beer!

By July, 1942, the fixed defences of Plymouth with the areas covered by fire from each battery were clearly defined and were to remain like that, with only minor alterations, for the rest of the war. The areas, shown on the wartime plan, were:

AREA "A". In respect of firing from Bovisand and Watch House Batteries and includes the sea area between 182 and 226 degrees to a radius of 8,000 yards.

AREA "B". In respect of firing from Watch House Battery and includes the sea area between 182 and 226 degrees to a radius of 20,000 yards.

AREA "C". In respect of firing from

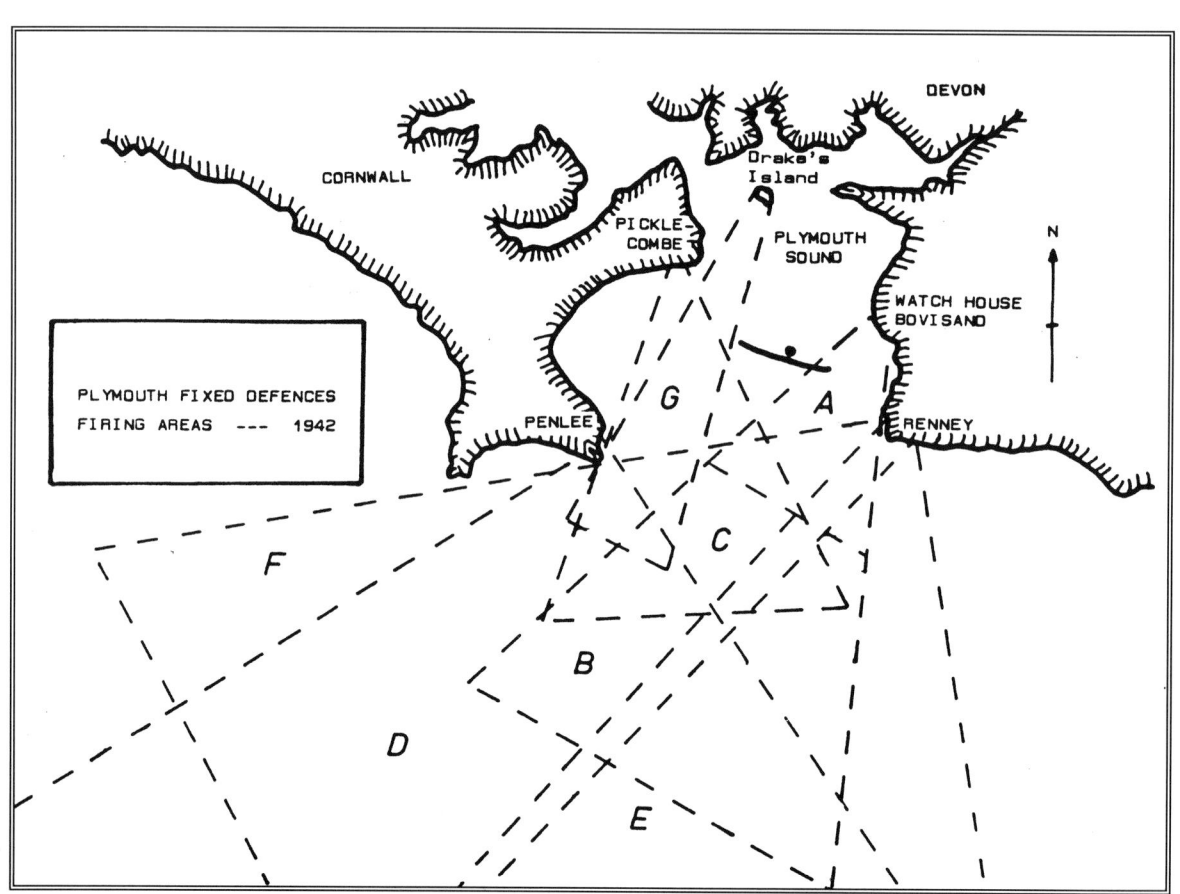

Picklecombe Battery and includes the sea area between 153 and 202 degrees to a radius of 14,000 yards.

AREA "D". In respect of firing from Penlee Battery and includes the sea area between 143 and 237 degrees to a radius of 30,000 yards.

AREA "E". In respect of firing from Renney Battery and includes the sea area between 168 and 220 degrees to a radius of 30,000 yards,

AREA "F". In respect of firing from Renney Battery and incljudes the sea area between 221 and 261 degrees to a radius of 30,000 yards.

AREA "G". In respect of firing from Drake's Island and Battery and includes the sea area between 193 and 209 degrees to a radius of 14,000 yards.

If there was no land attacks, air attacks continued throughout the years. Most were of the hit-and-run variety and these increased in 1943. The positions held by the coastal artillery batteries were often the best places for firing on these raiders. The Bren guns of Bovisand fired away, but they were not the best guns for such work. It wasn't until July 17, 1943, that they were given something bigger to fire at the German bombers.

Bigger it was, but whether it was better was hotly debated by the gunners. For the anti-aircraft "gun"supplied to Bovisand w.as a Projector U.P., 2-inch Naval pattern. Those who went through the London Blitzes might find that name strikes a chord. The projector in question was a crude form of rocket launcher, which could send up between four and six small rockets at a time. U.P. stands for "Unrotated Projectile", which again means that the rockets had no spin.

The ones used later in attempts to knock down German raiders and the V-1 flying bombs during attacks on London were very much larger and often manned by Home Guard batteries. After the warhead had exploded a large length of iron pipe with a venturi in the end was liable to hurtle back to ground. These were much prized by schoolboy souvenir collectors!

The larger London blitz batteries, mostly using American rocket projectors, were masterpieces of sophistication compared with that simple projector which was set up on the old No.2 emplacement of the 12-pounder battery between the demolished towers of the old top fort. However, it suffered from the same disease which attacked so many pieces of ordnance mounted at the fort - it was never fired in anger. Certainly there is no written record of the projector firing rockets at German bombers.

But a piece of weaponry that would be effective was on the way. In December, 1943, a quick-firing 40mm gun replaced the projector. That 40mm gun was better known as a Bofors, Highly-efficient, highly accurate, and with an extremely high rate of fire, the Bofors was one of the success stories of World War II. It took some time to set this one up on the site of No.2 emplacement, but it was finally ready to fire.

It first went into action on the night of April 30, 1944, pumping 66 rounds of highly-explosive shells into the night sky over the Sound. Whether it hit or damaged a German aircraft on that night or the many others when it opened fire is not recorded. But at least Bovisand was fighting back.

Shut That Door!

THE war was coming to an end. But this didn't stop Bovisand training recruits for the coast artillery units. The Coast Artillery Training Centre was not one unit, but was spread out between batteries at Brixham, Paignton, Ivybridge, Whitsand Bay and Bovisand.

After being called up, a recruit spent his first month like any other raw recruit in the Army with basic training. He then moved on to two months gunnery and specialist training. If he looked like officer material, he was sent to one of the many Officer Cadet Training Units (O.C.T.U.s), but otherwise he was like to find himself taking further training in artillery work at such places as Bovisand.

For Bovisand was now more of a training unit than anything else. The war was racing away into Germany and it was clear that the Fort would no longer be required to mount a defence against any German units. And at the end of 1944, this state of afffairs was recognised by placing the guns, mountings and associated stores into "care and maintenance"

The war ended and was celebrated by the firing of a number of blanks by the guns of Bovisand. In 1949, the district establishments of the Royal Artillery were replaced by independent maintenance batteries and the care and maintenance of Fort Bovisand was then carried out by C Troop, 261 Independent Maintenance Battery, R.A. This does not mean that Bovisand had fired its last. In fact, live ammunition was fired from all guns during that year. In 1950 both six-pounders were modified for high angle firing and new sights fitted. The same year new barrels were fitted to the guns.

In following years, the T.A. garrisoned the Fort for exercises and the guns continued to be fired. The largest of these exercises "Operation Widecombe Fair" which was designed to test the Fort's defences, involved nearly 10,000 men and was carried out in March 1955. Two years later, the Fort finished all operations and was handed over to the care of the Royal Engineers on March 14, 1957. This handover made the last entry in the Fort Record Book.

The last man out turned out the light by the main gate.

So the Fort closed down . Officially it was in the care and maintenance then of the Ministry of Defence. Which was a joke. But the M.O.D. were not to blame for the neglect which followed.

Imagine the number of staff needed to keep Bovisand ship-shape and Bristol fashion. It was quite beyond the means of the Ministry. Particularly so when you realised that Bovisand was just one of the forts they were being handed left, right and centre from all over the country. Some 23 forts and batteries had become redundant in the space of just a few years - and that's only counting the ones around Plymouth!

The "Services Correspondent" of one of the leading Devon newspapers put together a major feature about what was happening in those forts around Plymouth in February, 1963. He wrote:

"Most of them are now fighting a losing battle with decay and vandalism. But the War Office is quite firm. None is for sale - at present". Then he listed the condition of the forts, one by one.

"Bovisand Fort, fronting Staddon Heights, is gradually deteriorating into ruin. Its 30ft walls, 23 gun emplacements, and massive ironwork augmented by Portland cement, form a bastion which is gallantly defying the assaults of advancing years, the only enemy that has ever tested it.

"Nominally the War Department is still responsible for the fort although it has no further use for it. Both Admiralty and the R.A.F. have been asked whether they want it, but no decision has yet been made either way. The possibilty of developing the fort as a holiday centre has been discussed, but no firm plans can be made until the Service authorities make up their minds..."

It took the M.O.D. a long time to make up their minds. In the meantime the only visitors to the fort were unofficial ones - vandals and foxes. Feral cats took up residence and set up what amounted to colonies among the ruins. In those buildings even the vandals would not go.

Even so the damage those visitors did - the human ones - meant that all the non-ferrous metal was stripped out. So was a deal of the ironwork. Every pane of glass, no matter how small, was smashed. The weather took a hand too. South-westerly gales tore at the basic structure, ripping out any woodwork which had become rotten with damp. Rain pounded the roofs of the casemates exploiting every tiny crack and the Fort got damper and damper each year.

Even in hot summers, the Fort was not free from damage. A group of louts, destruction bent, decided to hasten matters by starting a fire in the upper part, the part of the Staddon Battery which had been completed in 1847 and had served as officers' quarters on and off over the years which followed the building of the casemates. The fire was a major one and left this part open to even more ruin from the weather in the next winters.

In the middle 1960's the Ministry of Defence decided that they were now open to offers. Not for an outright sale of the Fort, but certainly for leases. Many organisations became interested. Not many remained interested for longer than one committee meeting, but an exception was the British Sub-Aqua Club.

The BS-AC, the governing body for the sport of underwater swimming in Great Britain, in those same years was enjoying a tremendous boom in membership. Spurred on by films and tv, every young man, it seemed, wanted to become a Captain Cousteau and every girl a Lotte Hass.

The Club has, since its founding by Oscar Gugen and Peter Small in 1953, been a forward-looking organisation. The year of 65 was no exception. The Officers and Council of the Club looked forward to having their own H.Q. and National Diving Centre on the coast of Britain. When they heard about Bovisand, it sounded just the thing.

No time was lost. A small Comittee, headed by Alex Flinder, a well-known architect and Club vice-president, was set up to investigate the possibilities of making Fort Bovisand the British Sub-Aqua Club Diving Centre. They went to Bovisand. They probed about. And they returned with a report for the National Council.

I was a member of the Council at that time and I remember the vast enthusiasm for the idea of making the Fort our home. It had everything we needed - a small port of its own and almost limitless accommodation for divers. Discussions lasted deep into the night, but kept coming back to one or two hard facts.

First objection was that even with heavy grant-aid from the Sports Council, who had always helped the Club financially, the costs to us of putting the Fort back into shape, even stage by stage, were so enormous that even the most forward of us grew pale at the thought.

The second objection was one that could, most of us thought, have been overcome, but it was real. It concerned the fact that we would have to run the Fort from long-range. All the Officers and Council were, and are today, unpaid amateurs. All had jobs and no one could devote all the time that hands-on, on-the-spot control of the project would need. Yes, of course, we could have appointed a full-time manager. But that brought us back to money again.

So, with great reluctance, the Council had to turn the project down. Most of us believed that someone who could overcome our kind of difficulties would come along and make a huge success of it. But that time was not yet.

No one could know that the team who would do just that to Fort Bovisand had met three years before. In 1962, Lieutenant-Commander Alan Bax was on board H.M.S.Gurkha making her way through the Suez Canal when "the side of the Canal came out and hit her".

Alan Bax who had been qualified as a ship's diver earlier in his Navy service, went down under the ship to check the damage. He reported that the prop was bent, but not so badly that they could not move. And so his ship limped off to Karachi. Repairs were estimated to take a week. Which became a fortnight. Which became a month...

To fight the boredom, the Navy turned as it usually does to some form of sport. Karachi boasted, of all things, a rugby team. One of the players was called Jim Gill. Now Jim was an ex-Army man, who had served in both the American and British Armies (American father; English mother), and at the time Bax's ship was stuck in Karachi, he was working as an engineer for Caltex Oil.

"There was only one rugby team in Karachi - or for hundreds of miles roundabout - so we had to rely for opponents on any ships that came in," says Jim Gill..."The pitch was below high-tide level, but we played three times a week if we could find the opposition. It was a way of working up a thirst!"

There were other ways of working up a thirst. Someone taught the rugger players to play polo. "And then Alan offered to teach us to dive and took us all down to the beach for lessons," says Jim. "We did a lot of diving and I did a whole lot more after Alan left. We dived with mantas and sharks. Mind you, it's not particularly clear water there, but it is absolutely teeming with life".

Those diving lessons were to have a profound effect on the future of Fort Bovisand, but not for some time. Meanwhile Alan Bax carried on travelling with the Navy round the world. He was becoming more and more interested in the use of the aqualung as a tool for the archaeology of long-lost ships. Many of the divers he met on his voyages saw diving as something more than the opportunity to recover lost treasures. They saw another opportunity - to recover some of man's knowledge of his seafaring past.

The Bovisand story now switches to the Shetlands. In 1964, H.M.S. Shoulton visited the wreck site of a Dutch East Indiaman, De Liefde, lost in the Out Skerries, about 15 miles north-east of Lerwick, in 1711. The Naval divers dived and found a cannon and two silver coins.

In the Spring of 1965, John and Peter Bannon, together with a friend, Michael Harrison, formed an expedition to search for another Dutch East Indiaman, the Kennermerland, sunk in the Skerries in 1664. To this expedition the Bannons added two experienced Service divers - Lieutenant-Commander Alan Bax and Royal Marine officer, Malcolm Cavan.

Alan Bax dived the site first, but despite underwater viz of over 20m could see nothing and find nothing but rocks under a carpet of kelp. Malcolm Cavan then dived in a different spot. Within two minutes he was back on the surface, waving wildly. The first thought of those in the boat was that he was in trouble, but as they brought the boat over to him, they could hear what he was shouting: "I've found it, I've found it!" The proof was in his hands - two silver coins. But what he had found was not the Kennermerland, but the De Liefde of 1711.

After that re-location of the site, expedition after expedition went to the wreck, mapping, measuring, recovering items of shipboard life in centuries past, and recovering large quantities of silver coins.

In 1967, Alan Bax met Jim Gill once again. This time they met through the former captain of H.M.S.Gurkha, who lived near Jim who had now settled back in England. One meeting led to another, which in turn led to them diving together on the De Liefde. Later Jim worked closely with the famous American underwater photographer Flip Schulke on a film of one De Liefde expeditions. The film became an underwater archaeology classic, teaching new divers of the need for careful recording before the lifting of any artifact from an ancient ship.

Alan Bax and Jim Gill were now a team both in diving and underwater archaeology. Together they formed the School for Nautical Archaeology, Plymouth (better known as SNAP). They both taught that serious underwater archaeology in British waters could be carried out, despite the views of the land-bound archaeologists of that time.. Their work on the De Liefde had taught them that - they carried out the first archaeological pre-disturbance survey of the site - and now they passed their knowledge on.

At first the SNAP courses were at weekends only. They were based on the Royal Citadel in Plymouth. They were held at weekends as Alan Bax was serving out the last few months of his Navy career, working in Whitehall in the London offices of the Hydrographer.

The courses were a great success and during this period if you spoke of underwater archaeology in the South-West you were talking about SNAP. The British Sub-Aqua Club realised the importance of these courses by giving SNAP a scientific bursary grant of £100 and were rewarded with the knowledge that more than 100 divers became students at the School in the first year.

In fact the competition from British divers for places on these courses was one of the things which convinced Bax and Gill that there was a place for a full-time diving school, which they could use for all kinds of diving training. All they were short of was the place!

The forts around Plymouth seemed to fit the bill. After all they were right on their doorsteps. Bax and Gill had already fixed the two basic requirements of the place in which they would open their diving centre. They were (a) that it must be near the sea, and (b) that it must be spacious enough for both diving gear for wet work and classrooms for dry. When they were considering the forts they narrowed their choice down to two - Fort Bovisand and Fort Picklecombe on the other side of the Sound.

Both had disadvantages. A property developer had tried to turn Fort Picklecombe into a holiday centre but the conversion costs brought that to an end before it was completed. Fort Bovisand had been turned down by the British Sub-Aqua Club on financial grounds.

Even so their ideas began to focus on Bovisand. It had a sheltered harbour of its own and a huge amount of space which could be turned into accommodation even if most of it was, at present, derelict.

Jim Gill was the key man here. An engineer, with another degree in art and architecture, he decided that Bovisand was not so far gone that nothing could be done with it. In fact he thought that something very good could be done with it. And so, the two men put their heads, and every penny they had got, together and decided to try and make a go of it. The limited company they formed was called Plymouth Ocean Projects. Alan Bax sank his £3,000 Naval gratuity into their dream and Jim Gill added his pay-off from Caltex in New York.

In 1970 Alan Bax retired from the Navy and on February 1 of that year, he and Jim Gill as P.O.P Limited signed a seven year lease on Fort Bovisand from the Ministry of Defence.

The Bax and Gill Show.

So Alan and Jim had Bovisand. The enormity of the task of putting the Fort into a decent state of repair doesn't seem to have appalled them as much as it would any ordinary house-buyer! But then they had a dream. They knew what the Fort could and would look like.

The dream, however, at that time must have seemed a long, long way from reality. Everywhere they looked was ruin. A wholesale rebuild was way beyond their resources. So they took it stage by stage, section by section.

The first chosen was the old armoury building, which until recently was the Fort's cafe and has now been turned back to accommodation. The casemates themselves were in a hideous state - all the glass was smashed, much of the woodwork, which closed the landward end of each was destroyed, the piping was torn out and even some of the coping stones were ripped off. You couldn't even walk up the road behind the casemates, you had to climb over rubble and debris.

But the old armoury was at least dry. And very soon the first diver-students arrived - a team of British Army soldiers from Germany. It was intended that they should sleep in the armoury. But they took one look and said "no way" and other words which sounded like its German equivalent, and were put up at a nearby caravan park!

More improvements were made, word got around and more students came. From July,1970, they stayed at the Fort. Where you eat now in the cafe, they slept in a dormitory. The food service area of today is where the lounge and eating area was, and there was a tiny kitchen at the back.

Next place to be tackled was Casemate 10, which became the first classroom. The areas which had escaped the most damage were the magazines under the casemates, some of which are now used as classrooms. Soon the lighting was restored - by buying a generator. And gradually, one by one, the casemates were repaired and turned into accommodation. Then the old dormitory in the present cafe became the Fort's first bar - a very essential piece of equipment for divers to this day!

One big hold-up to all the work was a shortage of water. The pipes were there, but no water reached the taps. It seems the last man out when the Fort closed down had not only switched off the lights, but had somewhere turned off the water. No one could find the stopcock so water had to be brought to the Fort from a supply near the Coastguard Cottages in new dustbins on the back of a lorry.

Jim found a drawing of the Fort dated 1932 showing the route of the water main, but as most of it lay under shrubbery and wasteland to the top right hand side of the Fort all searches for the elusive stopcock failed to find it.

Then they heard of a man who knew a man who knew a man who lived at nearby Turnchapel, who was called Fred and said that as he had looked after the

The rubble has been cleared, and so have the brambles, grass and gorse, which grew two feet high along the Fort's inner road. Alan Bax and Jim Gill have started work, though Casemate 11 is still open to wind and rain.

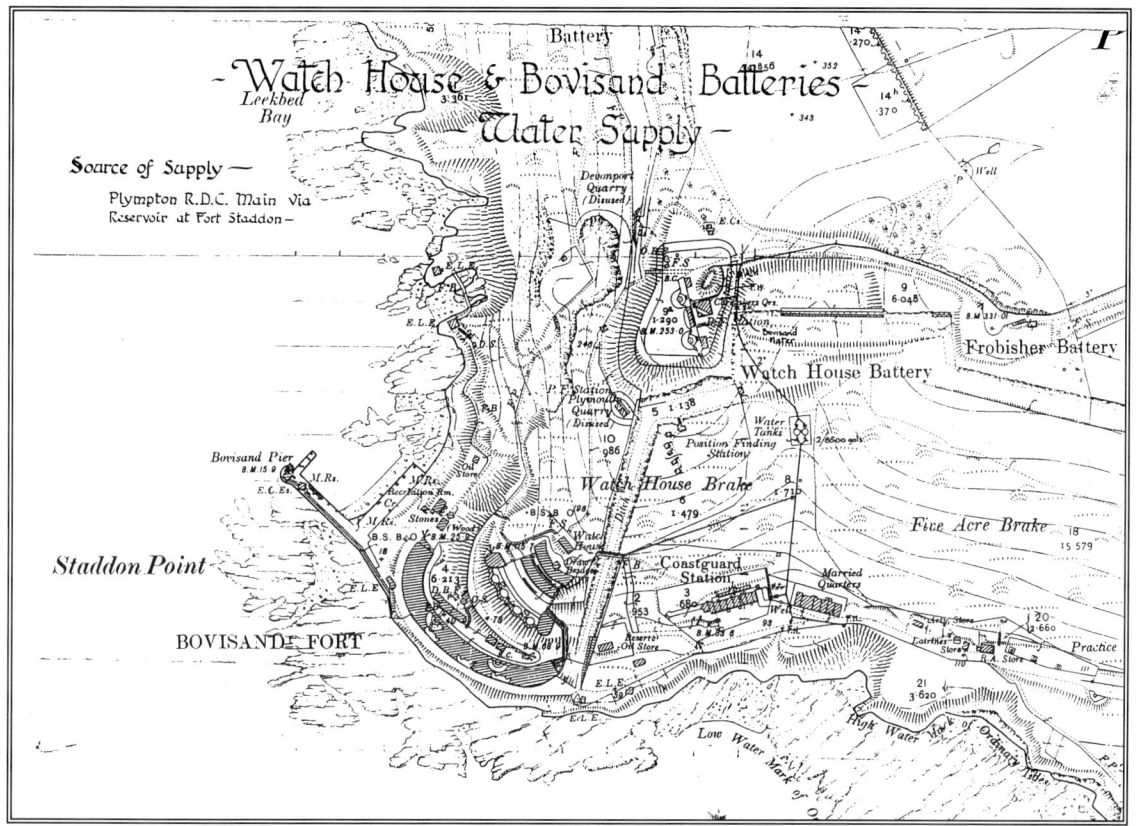

This is the plan which Jim found of the Fort's water supply.

Fort's water supply many years ago, he thought he could find the stopcock, given some help.

Help he certainly got. Alan and Jim almost carried him over the rough spots and into the jungle which covered the Fort's slopes. Finally the man stopped them. "Right," said Fred, "it's here". And there, buried in weeds under a bush, it was. Surprisingly the stopcock turned without too much effort. When Jim and Alan got back to the Fort, the water was back all right. It was spurting out of all the taps and out of many other places they didn't expect!

Most of the equipment concerned with the old guns in the casemates had disappeared long before. What had been left after the casemates were converted into barrack rooms, such as the traversing rings and bearing arcs let into the floor had long gone into the vandals' non-ferous-metal collection. But not all. Under the carpets of one or two of the casemates these signs of ancient gunnery still exist.

As a result of his building work, Jim Gill suspects that the original builders had their own brick "factory". He points out that every brick in the place seems to be different from its neighbour.

One of the early non-diving visitors to see the work

going on at the Fort was unexpected - the Fort's first commanding officer in World War Two. Then he was Lieutenant T.K.Hitchins of 157 Battery, Royal Artillery, now he is a retired agricultural merchant of Roborough, Plymouth. He was paying his first visit to the Fort since he left in 1940. But Mr.Hitchins has another claim to fame as far as the Fort is concerned. He proposed to his wife, Peggy, on top of the casemates, when she visited the Fort with a concert party to entertain the artillerymen stationed there in the early days of the war. They had known each other before this romantic meeting, but he actually popped the question in the moonlight overlooking the sea!

Alan Bax and Jim Gill.

Less romantic, of course, was the work that Jim Gill and his team had to do renovating the Fort. For example, the present stairway to The Pop Inn, the Fort's magnificent bar, which has the most interesting views of any bar in Britain, looking out over the Sound and the Breakwater, could not be put in place until a way had been blasted through with explosives.

Today's Reception is the magazine for the six-pounder guns which were mounted on the top of the casemates, hence the great iron doors at the entrance. Shell hoists ran up either side of the walls of the reception and the bar is on one of the six-pounder open gun platforms!

Work went on non-stop. Not all was simple. One of the casemates, No.18 in the old days, has an upstairs and downstairs. That too needed explosives to blast the floor out right to the top of the arches in the magazine to give the necessary depth.

Up the hill behind the old 12-pounder emplacements is the part of the old Fort, which was knocked into shape so that Devon County Council could run a marine centre there. Youngsters lived there in light and spacious dormitories while learning the arts of sailing and canoeing down in the harbour and Sound.

The marine centre is now self-catering accommodation for divers and is often booked up long in advance. These comfortable dormitories and private rooms cater for groups of between 10 and 40 people. They show no signs of the hellish hard work put in during the 70s to make it the place it is today.

Jim Gill will tell you about it. In one place they had to tunnel through ten feet of solid rock to make way for service lines. It was in this part of the fort that the vandals lit their fire years ago and which gutted the World War Two officers' mess and dining room. The chain for the drawbridge across the moat at the top was kept in a deep cavity, which could only be reached by a trap-door. It is now a larder in one of the kitchens of the self-catering section.

That was one of the hardest larders ever to be created. To open it up, a passageway had to be smashed through a solid stone wall. That larder was known for years as "Linda's Larder" because Linda Ashmore, wife of Bovisand's Nic Ashmore, smashed her way through using an electric kango hammer. It took her a week. But everyone on the staff of Bovisand then expected to work on the conversion during any free time they had from running diving courses.

While the Fort was slowly converted into a modern dive centre, divers had to be encouraged to use it. Without such use, there would be no more money for improvements. So getting divers to visit the Fort became Alan Bax's prime task. He was soon offering a vast array of courses to both amateur and professional divers. But offering new courses at the Fort was not enough. The courses had to be of high quality using the best of modern equipment. And they were.

Alan Bax travelled the country vising most of the amteur divers' branches, speaking at their dinners and "selling" the Fort whever he went. Soon these "sales tours" expanded into Europe and then the United States, As a direct result divers of many nationalities were soon sharing the Bovisand experience. The Fort's international reputation grew and grew and Alan Bax had his work recognised by the presentation to him of the PADI Special Award for Services to Sport Diving.

Success Story.

It is a far cry now back to those February days of 1970 when the work first started. Within two years, the Fort had classrooms, projection rooms, darkrooms, dive shop, hire centre, air supplies, workshops, accommodation, conference facilities, a bar, cafe, and a medical centre. As a result in March 1972, Alan Bax and Jim Gill thought the work advanced enough to hold an official opening! In the bar you will see a plaque to commemorate that opening ceremony conducted by Dr.Roger Bannister, then Chairman of the Sports Council, better known to millions as the first man to run a four-minute mile.

About this time P.O.P. asked for and got their lease extended by the M.O.D. from seven years to 21.

Some of the casemates were let to other organisations. A Fort Bovisand casemate, for example, is the home of the Joint Services Sub-Aqua Diving Centre, which is run by the M.O.D for service personnel and provides them with recreational diving training for members of all the Armed Forces.

Fort Bovisand is the base too for the Government's Basic Air Diving Courses, which were originally funded by the Manpower Services Commission. The original courses at Bovisand were to train divers to work on Britain's North Sea oil rigs, but have more recently trained divers for commercial work of all kinds.

In fact the Fort made its first links with the world of commercial diving when Rick Wharton of Comex Aberdeen, approached Alan Bax for help. In 1981, Rick Wharton was to carry out one of the richest salvages of all time with the recovery of millions in Russian gold ingots from the strong room of HMS Edinburgh 600 feet down in the Barents Sea.

Rick Wharton was concerned at the shortage of trained divers for North Sea oil work and believing that the employment of unsuitable candidates was largely responsible for the rising losses of divers in the North Sea, asked Bovisand to screen would-be recruits before they embarked on a diving career in the oil industry.

John Bevan, one of the leading divers in Britain who had worked on experimental deep dives with gas mixtures during his time as the Head of the Environmental Factors Section of the Royal Naval Physiological Laboratory at Alverstoke, Hampshire, helped set the standards for the screening of would-be diving recruits and brought the first modern surface supply equipment to the Fort.

In the bar at Bovisand you will see elaborate logos, many of brass, dedicated to the Fort and their instructors by the BAD Lads as the first graduates from these arduous Basic Air Diving courses styled themselves. The name stuck and the Bad Lads are still passing through Bovisand and the Breakwater Fort to this day. Which means a new logo appears on the walls around the bar every six weeks! It also means that you are liable to meet "Dive Bovisand" T-shirts all over the world!

Work in the North Sea was tough and divers died. In

1972, the concern about North Sea fatalities was growing and new diving regulations(which became law in 1975) were set by the Manpower Services Commission. These rigorous regulations included new Diver Training Standards. Only three organisations in Britain were originally certified to teach to these standards - Fort Bovisand, Fort William in Scotland, and Pro-Dive in Cornwall.

The Basic Air Diving Courses at Bovisand qualified at least 3,000 divers up to commercial diving standards. Those who were trained at the Fort now work on projects all over the world, not all of which are oil diving operations.

Alan Bax and Jim Gill never lost their early enthusiasm for marine or underwater archaeology. SNAP was backed by Council for Nautical Archaeology, which in turn led to the Nautical Archaeology Society. Bovisand hosted the first international symposium of underwater archaeology in 1971 And Alan has continued to organise them at the Fort every year since then.

One of the earliest speakers was Margaret Rule who came to Bovisand to present the first of the Mary Rose lectures to the delegates at the Fort. Today all the great names of marine archaeology look upon the Fort as their spiritual home. These symposia attract the world's archaeologists in such numbers that the events are booked out as soon as the next year's date is announced.

In 1982, Dr.Maurice Cross, a specialist in Britain in the treatment and cure of decompression sickness (the "Bends") and other diving diseases, arrived at Fort Bovisand. With financial help from John Houlder, a major shareholder of Comex, a diving company which would benefit from advances in the prevention and treatment emerging from the centre's research, Dr. Cross built the Fort's medical centre up into the Diving Diseases' Research Centre, complete with three large recompression chambers.

In the years which followed these chambers (two of which came from *Oregis*, one of the first specially-designed diving support vessels owned by Comex) treated the vast majority of sport diving accident cases in Southern Britain. Its helicopter pad was in frequent use for casualties needing treatment in the Bovisand "pot"until 1996, when the D.D.R.C. moved its operation to a custom-built centre with big new chambers at the Derriford Hospital, Plymouth, where

Trainee learning to use commercial diving equipment

it not only deals with the "bends", but treats many common medical complaints with hyperbaric oxygen therapy.

The Medical Centre at Bovisand still has a chamber ready to deal with any urgent bend cases from the area, involving both commercial and sport divers.

In the very early days British Sub-Aqua Club branches would hire a coach, drive to Plymouth for a weekend's diving and be quite content with a sleeping bag on the floor of one of the casemates, decrying those who booked a bunk bed as "sissy"!

But though the sleeping areas were upgraded time and time again over the years, it was always clear that there was a need for first-class accommodation at the Fort.

In 1984, that need was met by the building of the "New Block", above and behind the medical research centre and overlooking the harbour.

It was in fact built on the site of the old World War Two NAAFI. And it was built by the Fort Bovisand team with some outside assistance.

"The reason that we built it," says Jim Gill, "is that when we put our designs out to tender they all came back two or three times more expensive than we could possibly afford". Jim consulted with "Artie" Shaw, an ex-Naval diving instructor and petty officer, who was the Fort's chief instructor and had been in charge of the commercial diving training at the Fort, before working on civil engineering contracts full-time. "Let's build it ourselves", said Artie. And so they did.

Work on building 20 bedrooms in the "New Block" is underway.

Steel fixing to reinforce the huge retaining wall needed to hold back the hillside behind the new building was the main problem. But despite one fall of earth which buried their excavator overnight, the work was completed in reasonable time.

Jim Gill designed the new block. He is an architect and an engineer (and holds a Southampton University degree in education). The block was to have 20 rooms, ten on each of two levels. The rooms were aimed at the diver, who had grown, or aged, out of the rough, tough diving of his early underwater days and now thought diving should be more comfortable. They were an instant success and provide marvellous views of all the activity in the Sound.

The cost of building the block was helped by a grant from the English Tourist Board, but Jim reckons that if you had charged the project with the real costs

Fort Bovisand's specially adapted barge for deep water wet bell diving is moored at Barn Pool.

of all the work of those who took part, you would have been looking at a bill for £250,000!

Jim Gill's wife, Rhoda, became Hotel and Catering Manager of the Fort in 1980. Jim and Rhoda live at Turnchapel where Jim can keep an eye on his beloved motor yacht, built in 1928 and a classic example from the vintage years of British pleasure boat building.

Commercial diving training requires deep water, deeper than that available around the Breakwater Fort, on the seabed around which many basic commercial skills are taught to the trainees. So the Fort keeps a specially adapted barge moored in Barn Pool under Mount Edgcumbe. A wet bell is operated from this barge, but even the 33metres under that mooring is not sufficient to teach other deepwater skills. To find water even deeper for further training, at certain times on each course, the barge and bell are towed by tug over to a mooring off the Royal William Victualling Yard where over 40m of near nil-visibility water is guaranteed!

The tug is hired to tow the barge across as the Fort has found this more efficient than running their own fleet of workboats. British Diver, the former BSAC National Diving Boat, which was once operated by Fort Bovisand for amateur divers, was sold in 1986 and for some years was used as a floating classroom for marine students of Plymouth.

On Wednesday August 21,1996, after nursing Bovisand for 26 years and turning it from a derelict fort into the best-known diver training establishment in the world, Alan Bax and Jim Gill decided that it was time to hand over the main throttles powering the Fort and its future development to younger hands. They remain as directors, but Plymouth Ocean Projects is now controlled by a new Management team.

Regular visitors to Bovisand will know several members of the new board of management. Dave Welsh, who is now the owner of Plymouth Ocean Projects and is the Chairman and Managing Director of the company, was part of the original management team for the past four years. He was then head of marketing and special developments, one of which directly benefited divers by finding a way though the maze of regulations regarding funding for professional development so that course fees could be lowered. It is very appropriate that Dave Welsh is himself a graduate of an HSE Part III commercial diving course at the Fort! A veteran amateur diver of years before that, he has dived many of the wrecks around Bovisand. His wife, Wendy, is a diver too.

His plan for the future of Bovisand is to use the Fort and its facilities to bring diving more within the realm of the general public. He feels that diving is becoming known as a rich man's sport and he wants it to be within the pockets of everybody.

To that end the Fort has bought more equipment for hiring out so that someone who wants to dive from there does not need to have all their own equipment. He also wants to develop a bigger social side to the Fort's activities, making Fort Bovisand Club membership available to divers all over the country.

At the start of 1997, in a general upmarketing of the Fort's facilities, the Fort's cafe, (opposite Casemates 9,10 and 11) which in wartime was the Armoury, has now been converted to an accommodation block, complete with showers and toilets.

The new cafe is now more of a light and airy

Commercial Diver and Chairman: Dave Welsh.

restaurant than a cafe, and is suitably called the Dining Room, and occupies with the new kitchen, three casemates next to Reception, Nos.13,14 and 15. The huge gun hanging over your head in the dining room is not original Bovisand armament, but comes from a World War Two armed merchant cruiser! Casemates 16 and 17 are now a splendid conference room, which provides a bigger venue for the archaeological symposium and other large meetings.

Members of the new board of directors are Peter Sieniewicz, who has been Training Manager since 1992 and David Carter, Accounts Director, who now joins the company from the Diving Diseases Research Centre team when they were at Fort Bovisand and before their move to Derriford Hospital.

Alan Bax will stay on the board as Operations Director, which involves overseas developments and in-house proceedures and planning. He and his partner, Jill Williams, a retired university don, live in one of the old twin 6-pounder emplacements on the roof of the Fort. Jill is responsible for the landscaping and garden developnent of the Fort, and also manages the Fort's Publication Department. .

The civil engineering division, headed by Jim Gill, who also remains as a director, has become a separate part of the Fort's operations with Andy McGoldrick as Contracts Director. A new office for this part of the Fort's operations has been built into the hillside just off the road through the Fort which runs up to the Staddon Battery. This is officially called the Marine Engineering Contracts Office.

This division has has proved an extremely valuable diversification and makes a major contribution to the the Fort's income. The creation of this side of the Fort's operations started many years ago. Jim Gill says it came about because "if we were training more divers for commercial work and training them better, there was no reason why we shouldn't have an option on hiring the best ones to carry out commercial diving for us".

Work started in a small way in 1975 with a contract to drill and blast a pipeline trench across the River Plym for the South-West Gas Board and grew steadily. In 1976-79 the Plymouth Ocean Projects team carried out work for Kier Ltd at the Devonport Dockyard, including the nuclear complex. Their skills were soon in demand at sites around the world as well as those much nearer home. But they found time to build the new accommodation block at Fort Bovisand between other work in 1984.

Today they are a very substantial operation indeed. In 1995, for example, the Bovisand divers completed a large contract in Sutton Harbour. In 1996 another contract involved clearing four ammunition barges, sunk in the River Tamar in 1942. The divers lifted tons of badly corroded ammunition ranging from small arm rounds to large naval shells and depth-charges containing 300lb of high explosive, before raising the barges themselves.

The new owners of Plymouth Ocean Projects now have a 99 year lease of the Fort. This came about after a violent storm in 1991 sent huge seas crashing over the roadway leading down the side of the Fort and brought much of the road crashing to the rocks below. The damage was worst at the bend where the casemates of the Fort turn inland below the Coastguard Cottages. The lease of the Fort did not make the lessees responsible for repairs and the Ministry of Defence found themselves facing a very large bill. To be fair they made a superb job of underpinning the road and widening it. But it is clear

Just part of the lethal load of one of the ammunition barges in the Tamar. This salvaged depth charge once contained 300lb of H.E.

that they learned their lesson. When the Fort asked for another extension of their lease, the M.O.D. gave way with alacrity - and offered a 99-year lease but one which made the lessees responsible for future repairs!

WHAT DIVERS SHOULD KNOW ABOUT THE SOUND:

There is a speed limit of ten knots in the Sound.

There are other restrictions on certain areas. The first one you will no doubt hear...

HMS Cambridge Firing Range.

This shore establishment at Wembury Point has firing areas which extend 15 miles to seaward. All gunnery training for the Royal Navy is carried out here. Normal firing times are 8.30am to 5pm Tuesday to Friday inclusive. When firing is in progress or about to start, three large red flags are flown at Wembury Point and across the Sound at Penlee Fog Signal Station. All vessels have normal navigation rights during this time, but any vessel making a slow way across the range, or stopped on it, can interrupt firing. Yachts and small boats are asked to keep within one mile of the shore when crossing the area and to keep to a steady course and speed.

The Degaussing Ranges.

There are two main ones. The first is to the east of Penlee Point and the other to the south of the Point. Naval ships use these areas three or four times a week. A small boat in the area could hold up their work. If diving near these places keep a sharp lookout for any ships wanting to operate there.

High Power Sonar Trials.

These do take place occasionally within the Port area. The Harbour Master tries to inform all concerned, but if you hear or your divers report any strange noises underwater, abandon diving at once and contact the Harbour Master for information.

Trials of explosives are sometimes carried out. Cover boats are always present and will tell you if diving should be abandoned.

Tides and Visibility in the Sound.

There are big and strong tidal streams in the Sound itself. Springs rise 15 feet and neaps 12 feet, but a southerly gale can raise that as much as two or three feet. Northerly winds have the opposite effect.

Generally, the tidal stream is about one-and-a-half knots, but it can reach nearly three over the Cremyll Shoal. In the Hamaoze two knots is not uncommon. Tides can be exceptionally strong between Drake's Island and Ravenness Point, an area known as the Bridge.

Slack water in the Sound is usually at high and low water and lasts for no more than 30 minutes.

Visibility is better on the flood slack, because the ebb tide brings down silt from Hamaoze and Tamar. Diving in the Sound goes on all year. Only heavy rain inland on Dartmoor and other high ground puts a stop to diving as the Tamar and other streams that exit through the Sound to the sea, bring down heavily coloured water from that local red Devon earth. Otherwise divers can find reasonable visibility and sheltered spots even in the worst weather. However, the waters of the Sound do not allow sunlight to penetrate more than four metres, so divers should expect to find sealife higher up in the Sound than the open sea.

However, poor visibility should not put divers off the Sound. Extraordinary finds have been made in even the murkiest water. For example, a diver in the River Tamar discovered a bronze cannon dated 1540. Or at least part of one as the breech end had been blown away, probably during firing. The cannon was very similar to those found on the Mary Rose.

Winds and Weather:

The winds, of course, rule the diving out of Bovisand. The following details are the general rule, but everyone knows that the weather can change within moments. Small boat cox'ns should be prepared for it to do just that!

South-westerly winds bring mainly cloudy, and what Devonians call "dampy" weather. These winds are often accompanied with periods of rain and strong winds, particularly in winter. Gales come most often out of the south-west and west and usually last for four to six hours or even less in the summer. Divers should note that when a gale dies down this does not mean that the windy weather is over. Gales can follow one another almost immediately. Series of gales have been recorded with speeds of over 90 knots – a hurricane on the Beaufort Scale.

North-west winds bring showers and bright periods. But take care – squalls often come at the same time.

Winds from between east and south bring warm and mainly dry periods in summer and very cold times in winter.

Winds from the west are the most common throughout the year and those from the south-east are the least frequent and the least persistent.

North-east winds are most common in spring.

Divers out in small boats should be aware that they may suffer the worst of the weather close in. This is due to the wind funnelling down off those apparently protective great headlands or spilling out from river mouths like the Sound. Wind speeds in these "funnel" areas can be 20 per cent higher than in areas only a short distance away.

Diving cox'ns should watch out for the development of cumulonimbus clouds. These indicate that squally showers are likely, perhaps with hail and thunder. Sudden changes of direction and dramatic increases in wind force will come with them, strong enough to get small diving boats into trouble.

Spring comes early to Bovisand, which must account for the mass migration of divers to the Fort at Easter! They know what they are doing - this part of the British coast enjoys the best of the spring weather and that of the summer.

The sun shines on most days. On average there are usually only five days in June, July and August on which there is no sun at all. Over the same period temperatures on the south coast are between 18 and 20C.

The whole area enjoys higher temperatures than normal, but once again the wind affects it. South-westerly winds in summer cause a fall in temperature to slightly below average. A north-west or north-east wind will not affect the temperature, but an east or south wind will boost the warmth considerably. The air is slightly colder than the sea from October to March and slightly warmer from April to August. In September air and sea seem to match.

Thunderstorms are common during warm spells in the summer. It is odd to note that these storms usually form over France and drift north during the night before bursting forth after the dawn on Devon. The importance of this to the diver is that in such periods sudden squalls sweep across the sea inshore and there are sometimes waterspouts swirled up from the sea.

Fog is always a great hazard for small diving boats and is most common in spring and summer. This is because the mild westerlies are then blowing over the colder waters of the sea. Fogs can persist for two or three days but usually last only for 6-10 hours.

Keen night divers should note that in summer fog often drifts in after sunset. Fogs are most likely when the wind veers westerly. Then fog spreads across the whole area. Winds from the south also produce fog, but because the wind is less moist the fog is least over the eastern part of the area. In south-west wind conditions extensive banks of fog may form at any time of the year.

The Code for Bovisand Divers:

When the "A" Flag is flown at the Fort, it shows that diving operations are in progress in some part of the Bovisand areas, entrance channel or harbour.

There is a Bovisand Code of Conduct aimed at safety and the preservaion of wildlife and archaeological material in the immediate vicinity of the Fort. The following rules should be observed:

a) Power boats should enter and leave the harbour by the approach channel at all times.

b) The speed of boats in the approach channel and

harbour must not exceed four knots.

c) Permission must be obtained from the Training Office on weekdays between 8.30-5.30, otherwise the Hire Centre for:
1) Any diving in the harbour area and approach channel or diving areas, whether for sport, training or trials.
2) Mooring in the harbour.
3) Use of jetty steps, ladders or slip, for loading, unloading or launching.

Generally diving in the harbour area and approach channel should be kept to a minimum. Priority will be given to divers under training and trials groups.

d) Divers swimming in the Fort Bovisand diving areas should remain on the surface until they are well clear of the harbour and approach channel.

e) All diving groups in the area are to be clearly marked by a buoy carrying the diving flag and where possible this flag should be of a rigid material. SMB's are provided free by the Fort on a refundable deposit.

f) No conventional swimming is allowed from any part of the jetty.

g) No wildlife is to be collected from above or below water in the Bovisand areas without the permission of the Directors of Fort Bovisand. No spearguns to be carried or used.

The code also asks divers in the Plymouth area to take only that required for the use or consumption of the individual. It also asks them to report any archaeological finds thought to be more than 100 years old to the Directors.

When Divers Meet Fishermen:

The Bovisand Code of Conduct for divers has sensible advice for all Devon divers:

"The reality of the fishermen's use of the Plymouth area should first be understood. The only conflict of interests which is likely to occur is between divers and shell fisherman, of whom there are many full-time skippers in this area. They are likely to visit any given spot only a dozen or so times a year and then leave their gear down for a maximum of about 48 hours. Two types of gear are used:
a) The conventional lobster or crab pot.
b) Tangle nets. These are vertical nets with their bottoms on the seabed. They are some 2m high with a mesh of 20-25mm.

"Both types of gear are laid in lines which may be up to four or five hundred yards long and are marked with a float at each end.

"In view of this – the fact that the skippers and their crews rely on the sale of their catch for their livings and the fact that the tangle nets provide a very real danger to divers, all divers are asked to comply with the following rule:

"Do not dive between the buoys which mark each end of a net or pot line, nor close to the end markers.

"The local fishermen, in their turn, have agreed both to mark their floats or buoys with the registered number of their boats, and also to use buoys of such size that they are readily identifiable from one end of the line to the other.

"Remember, when you see one, look for the other – it may be several hundred yards away – and then do not dive between them."

Fish and Shellfish - the Rules:

If you wish to take fish or shellfish for your own supper during any dive, you must conform to the same rules as those which apply to professional fishermen, such as minimum fish sizes. Such rules are laid down by the Devon Sea Fisheries District in the form of bye-laws.

The western limit of the Devon Sea Fisheries District is oddly enough in Cornwall at "a line drawn true south from the seaward extremity of Rame Head in the County of Cornwall". The Sea Fisheries district does not extend above a line drawn across the mouth of every river, or stream flowing into the sea, or estuary. In Plymouth Sound for example, this means in the case of the Tamar, a line drawn across the river true south-east from the southernmost point of the Quay at Cotehele, another drawn across the Tavy along the sill or crest of the weir at Lopwell, and yet another across the Plym along the seaward side of the Laira Bridge at Plymouth.

Devon Sea Fisheries lays down minimum sizes of fish, which may be landed and these rules do apply to divers. They are, in centimetres:

Cod	**35**
Conger	58
Haddock	**30**
Hake	30
Plaice	**25**
Pollack	30
Witches	**28**
Lemon soles	25
Soles	**24**
Turbot	30
Brill	**30**
Megrims	25
Whitings	**27**
Dabs	15
Bass	**36**
Saithe	35
Herrings	**20**
Mackerel	20

Shellfish	mm
Scallops (across flatshell)	100
Edible crabs (across back)	
Males (cock)	160
Females (hen)	140
Lobster (carapace - base of rostrum spines to rear of body shell)	85
Spider crab (carapace - base of rostrum spines to rear of body shell)	120

There are three Acts of Parliament which affect the wreck diver:

Merchant Shipping Acts:

The Receiver of Wreck is responsible for the administration of the Merchant Shipping Act 1894 and the Merchant Shipping Act 1906 which deal with wreck and salvage. It is a legal requirement that all recovered wreck (flotsam, jetsam, derelict or lagan) whether recovered within or outside United Kingdom territorial waters is reported to the Receiver. Finders who conceal items can be prosecuted, so any object should be declared as soon as possible.

Wreck which remains unclaimed at the end of a one-year period becomes the property of the Crown and the Receiver is required to dispose of it. This may be by sale at auction, although in many cases the finder will be allowed to keep unclaimed items in lieu of a salvage award. However, this is at the discretion of the Receiver and each case is judged on its merits.

The Receiver of Wreck can be contacted at The Coastguard Agency, Spring Place, 105, Commercial Road, Southampton SO15 1EG. Tel: 01703-329474; fax: 01703-329477.

Military Remains Act:

This Act became law on September 8, 1986, and in the future may affect the wreck diver much more than it does at present. The main drive of the Act is to protect the sanctity of "war graves", that is the wreckage of military ships and aircraft known to contain human remains of service personnel.

The wreckage of all military aircraft of any nation is automatically protected, but Naval ships will have to be designated by the Secretary of State and will need a statutory instrument to do so. This means that ships will have to be named and approved by Parliament in the same way that ships to be protected as historic wrecks need a statutory instrument passed through Parliament.

There seems no doubt that those who passed the Act had little idea of the number of ships which could fall under its terms, such as a merchant ship with a naval gunner aboard - was he among the survivors? - and as a result no ships have yet been named under the Act. This does not mean that ships are not covered by the general thrust of the Act and divers should therefore treat all possible "war graves" with total respect.

However, once these ships have been named, the diver commits an offence only if he or she tampers with, damages, moves, removes, or unearths remains, or enters an enclosed interior space in the wreckage. Nothing in the Act prevents the wreck diver from visiting the site, examining the exterior or even settling on the wreckage. An offence is only committed if he or she disturbs remains or enters a proper compartment in the wreck. The punishment on conviction of an offence is a fine.

Protection of Wrecks Act:
Divers who find a site which they think might be of historical, archaeological or artistic importance should leave everything undisturbed and report their find, in confidence, to the Department of National Heritage. If appropriate, the wreck can then be designated under the Protection of Wrecks Act of 1973 to allow proper protection of the site.

Designated sites may only be dived or items recovered if a licence for that purpose has been granted. If a diver does so without permission, he or she commits an offence and can be fined. More information from The Secretariat of the Advisory Committee on Historic Wreck Sites, 3rd Floor, Department of National Heritage, 2/4, Cockspur Street, London SW1Y 5DH. Tel: 0171-211-6367/8

Further Reading:
Dive South Devon by Kendall McDonald (Underwater World Publications). Dive South Cornwall by Richard Larn (Underwater World Publications). Shipwrecks of the South Hams by Kendall McDonald (Wreckwalker Books). Marine Animals of the South West by Paul Naylor (Sound Diving).

Section TWO.

Diving Sites inside the Breakwater.

Admiralty charts:
- 95   (Wembury Bay and River Yealm);
- 1613 (Eddystone Rocks to Berry Head);
- 1900 (Approaches to Plymouth);
- 1967 (Plymouth Sound).

Sites are detailed anti-clockwise from Bovisand Harbour.

Fylrix British motor vessel.
Sunk: November 22, 1984. Capsized after cargo shift.
Position: 50 21 05N; 04 07 30W.
Depth: 5m.

Diving is banned on this 637-ton British motor vessel which is on her starboard side in Plymouth Sound. As she is in only 5m of water in Jennycliffe Bay, her whole side dries at low tide and she breaks

Members of an explosives course on the hull of the Fylrix.

surface at half-tide. She is 203ft long with a beam of 28ft. She is now used as a site for explosives courses.

The Fylrix was on her way from Dean Quarry at Porthoustock on the Lizard in Cornwall, with a load of granite chippings destined for London's roads. Many divers will know Porthoustock as the beach from which their dives on the Manacles have begun. During the Fylrix's voyage, a gale caught her off the Eddystone during the night of November 21, 1984 and in the big seas her cargo shifted and she developed a pronounced list to starboard. Her Master radioed for help and headed for Plymouth. He was escorted into the Sound by a Royal Navy frigate and anchored in the shelter of Jennycliffe Bay. During the early hours of the morning the list grew worse and the entire crew abandoned her just before she capsized.

Since then the Fylrix was visited by hundreds of amateur divers and she has been stripped of all possible souvenirs. The bronze propellor has gone. Before the diving ban was put into operation an amateur diver died when trapped inside the wreck.
WARNING:Explosives training site.

Cattewater Wreck . 14th Century Merchantman .
Sunk: January 17,1494. "In great winds"
Position: 50 21 41N; 04 07 37W. Just off R.A.F. Mount Batten.
Depth: 10m.
WARNING: Protected Historic Wreck.
No diving is allowed within 50m of that position. The Cattewater, which means "ship water" and presumably a mooring place in ancient times, is the last reach of the River Plym before it flows out through Cobbler Channel into the Sound proper.
The wreck was discovered when a dredger brought up wood when deepening the area around the old flying boat moorings. Parts of two small breech-loaders were brought up at the same time. A third gun was later raised by divers. By a process of elimination of ship wrecks recorded in Plymouth archives, there seems a strong possibility that this wreck is of the *St James of the Croyne* which sank "in great winds" during the night of January 17, 1494.

Promenade Pier, The Hoe
Depths: 9m
Nothing shows above water today, but in 1884, it was a very grand affair - 420 feet long with a ballroom and restaurant supported on 140 columns. German bombs and salvage work took it all below surface. Bottles, coins and bits and pieces of slot machines are found by divers. A compass course of 220 degrees from the Hoe Road steps will bring you to the wreckage.

The Walls.
Depths: To 40m.
You will find these sheer rock cliffs almost beneath the Longroom in Firestone Bay. Covered with jewel and plumose anemones and deadman's fingers, these walls plunge to just over 40m at their base.

Devil's Point.
Depths: To 38m.
These rock walls are a continuation of those in Firestone Bay and are similar except that you need to hug the face of the wall more closely. This is because you are becoming exposed to the strong tides of the Narrows and might be swept out into the main shipping channel.

Mashford's Shoal.
Depths: To 20m.
When all other sites are out because of weather, local divers switch to a rummage dive on this muddy site, which is named after the famous boatyard at Cremyll. Until the completion of the Breakwater in 1844, this was one of the most sheltered anchorages for shipping and heavily used by ships of all kinds. So

the debris of centuries lies in the Mashford mud. Many old bottles have been recovered by divers. Not all recoveries are so small, one local diver found a complete hard-hat diving helmet there.

The edge of the shoal ends in a wall of mud down to the stony ground of the main channel. Divers report that old timbers emerge from the wall and disappear just as quickly suggesting that there is a really old ship in the mud there.

Battery Bay.
Depths: To 40m.
At Wilderness Point. A cliff face dive dropping down to 40m. Very tidal, best dived on slack half-an-hour before High, when you have a 45-minute "window".

Barn Pool.
Depths: 7m to 30m.
Almost, but not quite, a shore dive on the banks of the Mount Edgcumbe Country Park. Take care, Fort Bovisand have a commercial-diver training platform moored nearby.

Barn Pool has been an anchoring place for boats for centuries, which means that there are interesting items to be found on the bottom. The water increases rapidly from 7m to 30m as you move offshore. At 30m and balanced almost on the edge of another drop into the main channel is a World War Two barge, possibly an ammunition carrier. The site is part of a Plymouth University project.

Drake's Island.
Depths: To 6m.
At 50 21 30; 04 09 10, this used to be known as St Nicholas Island. A prominent island, with a peak height of 21m, it is surrounded by rocky ledges some of which dry at Low.

On the south-east corner among the ledges, there are traces, mostly cannonballs, of the wreck of the almost-new 70-gun HMS Conqueror, blown on to the rocky ledges during a violent gale on October 26, 1760. She was heavily salvaged at the time.

To the south-west of the island is the wreck of a steel barge of over 100 feet, which shows at full low. This is believed to be part of the wartime anti-submarine net barriers across the sound and the barge may have been a gate-vessel.

In 1972, a diver found a magnificent bronze cannon in very shallow water just off the island. Nearly five feet long, it was fully charged with ball. It has been identified as a light field gun of the reign of Frederick II of Prussia, and dated between 1752 and 1780. The gun may have been part of land defences of the island or lost in some other wreck, but no other wreckage or guns have been found on the site of the discovery.

Mallard Shoal.
Depths: To 30m.
A scenic dive when vis is good. Dive with care – you are on the edge of the main channel. A cliff face here, which drops from 20 to 30m, is said to be the home of many lobsters. Watch for ships coming out of the Cattewater via the Cobbler Channel. You may also find a sailing club mark here.

Asia Knoll.
Depths: To 12m.
A drift dive north of Drake's Island, but you must keep inside the marker of the main channel in depths of 10-12m. This is flatfish country. There is also a deal of rubbish on the bottom. Beware the ferries which sometimes take a short cut!

Die Fraumetta Catharina von Flensburg. Brigantine.
Sunk: December 10, 1786. Southerly gale.
Position: 50 21 06N; 04 09 46W.
Depth: 34m.

A bronze bell, shining bright green and poking out of the dark mud bottom of Plymouth Sound not far from Drake's Island led to the accidental discovery of this wreck by divers of Plymouth Sound BSAC in October 1973.

The night of December 10, 1786 threatened disaster for all the shipping then in Plymouth, for the wind that night was a southerly gale, blowing straight into the Sound. The Catharina had only arrived that day, seeking shelter from the worsening weather. She was on the way from St Petersburg (which we now call Leningrad) to Genoa, with a cargo of hemp and leather hides. At 10pm the wind broke the Catharina from her moorings, hurled the 53-ton brigantine on to the rocks of Drake's Island, then drove her across the foam-filled narrows towards Mount Edgcumbe, before she sank in the darkness under the Raven's Cliffs. Somehow the crew struggled ashore, but the ship went down in deep water.

The bell the divers raised bore the full name of the Catharina and the date 1782. From Flensburg in West Germany, the divers were able to establish that the ship had been built there, (then in Denmark), in 1782. Her owners were Hinrich Lorck and Knut Andersen and her Captain was Hans Jensen Twedt.

Further exploration of the wreck site turned up her anchor and a few rolls of leather. Each roll contained six complete reindeer hides, complete with tails and with Russian lettering cut into them. The silt had preserved the hide, assisted by tanning with willow bark and currying with birch oil. Since those first few discoveries, an archaeological survey by the Plymouth Sound divers of the site using airlifts, has revealed that there is 75 per cent of the ship below the mud and that her holds are packed with rolls of hides, hundreds of them!

So well preserved was the leather that shoes, handbags, brief cases, attache cases, belts, shoulder bags and doctors' bags have all been made from it. Sales of these have made it possible to fund a continuing excavation and provide the project divers with a hard dive boat.

The bell from the wreck was presented to Prince Charles, the British Sub-Aqua Club's President, at the Club's 21st anniversay banquet in London's Guildhall in November, 1974. Wrecks found in certain areas of the West Country become the property of the Duchy of Cornwall and Prince Charles is the Duke of Cornwall. But he relinquished his ownership in favour of Plymouth Sound BS-AC!

WARNING: Diving by those not in the Catharina project team is not usually allowed, but Ian Skelton, leader of the project, and Glen Peacham, the Plymouth Sound BSAC diving officer (01752-348773), will let other suitably qualified divers visit the wreck on a look-but-no-touch basis.

The bell of the Fraumetta Catherina von Flensburg sits on the top table at the BS-AC's 21st anniversary dinner in Guildhall in 1974. Harry Secombe introduces the Club to its new national anthem - "I'm forever blowing bubbles... - to the evident delight of Prince Charles, the Club's President.

Queen's Grounds.
Depth: 10m
Off Picklecombe Point and Fort Picklecombe, which is a western version of Fort Bovisand, but converted into flats, is a fine ground for flatties in less than 10m. It is essential to make sure that you do not drift dive into the main channel.

Plymouth Breakwater.
Depths: To 10m.

The actual breakwater is 1700 yards long. Diving on the southern edge provides depths down to 10m where the rocks and boulders of the wave-breaking material dumped to protect the actual construction gives way to a seabed of rough ground with sand, shale and rocky outcrops.

In 1993, a diver was exploring the area just off the Breakwater when a bright green glow told him that he was looking at a tube of brass. He thought at first that he had found a naval shellcase. Its weight told him it was more than that. In fact, he had discovered a two-foot long brass gun made, according to the inscription on it by a well-known gunfounder "Thomas Pyke of Bridgwater" and dated 1787. It was on its own, lying in the open on the seabed and not apparently associated with any wreckage.

Even so it probably means that a wreck of a slightly later date is somewhere close by.

Plymouth Breakwater Lighthouse. At the west end of the Breakwater. The tower is 23m high, with the height of the light 19m above mean High Water. It has a range of 15 miles, with a white and red flash every ten seconds.

The remains of a Sunderland Flying Boat, which crashed on landing in fog on March 13, 1942 is scattered on the seabed between the lighthouse and the Breakwater Fort on the inside of the Breakwater. One of the five passengers killed on this flight from Gibraltar, Captain F.T.Peters, R.N., was awarded a posthumous V.C. for his actions earlier during "Operation Reservist", a daring penetration by Navy ships of Oran Harbour to stop the Vichy French sabotaging the port before the Allied landings.

Breakwater Beacon. A conical light beacon with a black framework ball topmark 15m high at the east end of the Breakwater. The topmark is meant to be a refuge for shipwrecked sailors and can take six people. There are stone shelters – four – at intervals along the Breakwater and the landing pier is mid-way on the north side.

Breakwater Fort
Depth: To 15m.

This fort is 50yds north of the centre of the Breakwater and there is 7.3m of water in the passage between them. Depths around the Breakwater Fort, which is extensively used for commercial diver training by Fort Bovisand which holds a lease on it, vary from 12m to 15m.
. The Fort is 144ft long and 114ft wide. It was planned to have two storeys of iron and to house fourteen 12.5in guns and four 10in guns. It soon became obsolete and spent most of its early life as a Naval signal station.

Hopper Barge No.42. Steam-engined barge.
Sunk: September 13,1913. Bad navigation on dark night.
Position: 50 20 06N; 04 09 30W.
Depth: 15m.

On September 13, 1913, this 150-ton self-propelled barge was returning from a Spanish dredging contract at Corunna, when she smashed into the Plymouth Breakwater and ran up on to it. The eight men of the crew got off safely. The barge was towed off, but sank. She is now in two parts. To the north-west lie her boiler and firebox; to the south-west is most of the upturned barge, though a large part of it is buried under the sand seabed in 15m. **Warning:**

Hopper No.42 ran right up on the Breakwater before sinking.

This wreck is in the main shipping channel and like all diving in the Sound needs special permission from the Queen's Harbour Master to dive her.

Lancaster ED 450 G. R.A.F. Heavy bomber.
Crashed: February 14, 1943. Damaged on bombing mission.
Position: 50 19 58N; 04 09 10W.
Depth: 15m.

Returning from a raid on the U-boat pens at Lorient in Brittany, this Lancaster Mark III, ED 450 G, piloted by Flight Sgt. G.B.C.Miller, of 49 Squadron RAF, is believed to have been so badly damaged that he was trying to make a landing anywhere. He took off from Fiskerton, Nottinghamshire, at 7pm on February 13, 1943. And in the early hours of the next day hit the steel cable of a barrage balloon protecting shipping in Plymouth Sound. The aircraft crashed almost on to the Plymouth Breakwater. The bodies of the seven crew were never found and they may all have baled out over the sea some time earlier. Today the wreckage is mostly in small pieces, though engines are recognisable, and is scattered among the blocks of the Breakwater at the western end of the seaward side in 15m. An aircraft recovery group raised one of the Rolls Royce engines, a propellor and other pieces.

Yvonne. Four-masted barquentine.
Sunk: October 3, 1920. Southerly gale.
Position: 50 20 00N; 04 08 15W.
Depth: 9m.

The Yvonne of over 1,000 tons, home port Marseilles, left Jamaica early in August, 1920 with a cargo of wood for Le Havre. On October 3, in the early evening, a southerly gale dashed the Yvonne of over 1000 tons on to the Plymouth Breakwater's eastern end. Eighteen of her crew were saved by scrambling on to the Breakwater and over it to the Plymouth lifeboat. But one man, the cook, was lost. Today, the little that is left of the Yvonne is at the bottom of the Breakwater a short distance to the west of the eastern beacon. Most prominent item is her big anchor and chain at 9m among the blocks of stone placed there to break the force of the waves striking the Breakwater itself.

HMS Abelard. Drifter Minesweeper.
Sunk: December 24, 1916. Possibly hit mine.
Position: 50 19 53N; 04 08 27W.
Depth: 10m.

Abelard was a 187-ton steam trawler built in 1909 in North Shields. She was requisitioned by the Navy as a drifter-minesweeper at the start of the 1914-18 War. On Christmas Eve, 1916 she was wrecked "two cables 240 degrees from the Breakwater Beacon" and her masts stuck up eight feet above the water at low springs.

Salvage operations started at once, but by January 11 were postponed and then abandoned. There was talk that she had hit a mine, but there is no conclusive evidence of this.

Well broken, her bows face south and her boiler stands 5m proud of a sandy seabed in 10m. The iron propellor is still to be seen. The rest of the flattened wreckage lies among boulders and kelp.

Section THREE.

Sites outside the Breakwater.

> **Admiralty Charts:**
> 1613 (Eddystone Rocks to Berry Head)
> 1900 (Approaches to Plymouth)
> 1967 (Plymouth Sound)

Two Trawlers
Sunk. Date not known
Position: 50 19 42N; 04 10 14W
Depth: 15m.

Little is known about the remains of these two trawlers, whose wreckage stands 4m high in 15m. They were probably World War Two casualties or used to open and close nets at entrances to the Sound during that war. Some salvage or dispersal was carried out in 1946.

WARNING: Wreckage is reported to be heavily netted.

Encourage. Motor Fishing Vessel.
Sunk: October 25, 1940. Parachute mine.
Position: 50 19 25N; 04 09 57W
Depth: 12m.

This 45 ton MFV sank after hitting a mine on October 25, 1940 while leaving Plymouth for the fishing grounds. The crew of four were lost. The mine is believed to have been one of many dropped by parachutes from German aircraft. The fishing boat's mast was visible at Low Water for some time "6.5 cables from the Breakwater Fort 210 degrees", but she is now totally broken up with little more than a few timbers and her engine block remaining in 12m.

Poulmic. French Transport.
Sunk: October 6, 1940. Parachute mine.
Position: 50 19 05N; 04 09 38W.
Depth: 20m

Another victim of a parachuted sea mine, this

Manned by the Free French when a parachute mine blew her apart.

French transport ship of 350 tons was in Plymouth when France surrendered in 1940 and was taken over by the Royal Navy. Manned by the Free French forces she was used as a patrol vessel.

The 122ft ship, with a beam of 27ft, could do 12 knots and was being used as a minesweeper in the entrance to Plymouth Sound off Penlee Point when she struck a mine herself. The ship was literally blown apart. The largest section is her double bottom. Deck winches are to be seen, as are parts of her engine. Highest point of the wreck is a rib which stands 5m high on a rocky seabed varying from 15-20m. There are many Oerlikon anti-aircraft shells lying around in the gullies in a bad state of preservation and they should be considered dangerous. There are one or two larger shellcases amid the wreckage – and two large cannon balls which appear to be practice shots dating from the big guns of the early days of Fort Bovisand or Fort Picklecombe.

Coronation. English man o'war of 90 guns.
Sunk September 2, 1691. Capsized in "verry squally weather"
Positions: In two parts. Inshore site: 50 18 96N; 04 11 57W (no diving within 250m radius); Offshore site: 50 18 57N; 04 11 98W (no diving within 150m)
Depth: Inshore: 12m. Offshore: 20m.
WARNING: Protected historic wreck.

The loss of Coronation with nearly 400 men shocked Plymouth and when it became more widely known shocked the country too. It was not as if she had been a leaky old tub fit only to become a prison hulk. This was a fine ship, a pride of the Navy.

When she was launched at Portsmouth in 1685, she was listed as a second rate man-of-war of 1366 tons and carried a crew of 660 men to sail her and man her 90 cannon. One hundred and forty feet long with a beam of 44 feet 9inches, she drew 18 feet of water when fully laden.

And she was fully laden that September of 1691 when she was off Ushant ready for battle with any French ships that might dare to come out of Brest and face the English fleet. Coronation and other ships of the Fleet were just a week out of Torbay, hoping to draw the French fleet out to fight.

At first the weather was good and endless patrolling didn't seem too bad, but on Tuesday, September 1, the wind started to rise. "Squally weather verry fresh" noted the log-keeper of the Royal Oak, which had Coronation close by. Captain Charles Skelton of Coronation knew then that if the wind continued increasing, he and the other captains would soon have to abandon the patrol and seek shelter.

The Fleet finally turned for Plymouth in the early hours of the morning. The weather was going from bad to worse. The ships' logs now all had the same entry - "verry Squally Stormy weather" - as the big ships of the Channel Fleet strained, lurched and rolled towards Plymouth Sound, though the most experienced of their captains knew that real shelter would only come when they reached the Hamoaze. The Sound itself would be a stormy place in such winds. For the wind couldn't seem to settle in one direction. First it was coming from the south. Then it swung to the south-west, which helped them on their way, but finally settled in the south-south-east and increased to full gale. It was now a killer wind for any ship trying to enter Plymouth Sound.

The Northumberland ran for the entrance and made it, only to go aground in the entrance to the Hamoaze. The Harwich was next, but didn't get as far. As the full blast of the wind hit him inside the Sound, Captain Robinson of the Harwich realised the danger and let go his anchors. They didn't stop him and he was soon on the rocks near the entrance to the Hamoaze. A wreck, but not a total loss and all got ashore.

Luckier still was the Royal Oak. She ran fairly gently aground "under Mount Edgecumbe House" and later when lightened of her guns was able to be taken into the Dockyard for repairs.

The worst was reserved for last. Skelton brought his Coronation nicely in towards the entrance to the Sound. Dead centre and going well. But then a rogue squall caught her side on. For a moment watchers on the shore thought she was going to capsize. Huge waves battered her as she lost way and they probably started a massive leak below her lower gun ports. Later they were to say that his gun ports were not properly lined or caulked. Whatever the reason Coronation now took on a savage list.

Skelton must have felt the water below decks and realised that his masts were now the danger. His ship's carpenters were ordered to work and within moments the great masts toppled down; they did not need cutting right through, but snapped under own weight and the wind howling against them.

Nothing could now hold the ship off the rocks of Penlee Point, the most easterly part of Cornwall. She hit the seabed just off the Point and when she hit she rolled. For a moment those watching on shore saw her ensign staff standing and then she was gone. And gone with her were Skelton and a great number of her crew.

When the court-martial into her loss was held on October 22,1691 on board the Dutchess in the River Medway, the captains of the court decided that "by a Butt-head starting, or some Planke giving way Shee sprung a Leake and thereby was lost. And we doe not find that there was any Neglect or failure of Duty in Captain Skelton, Late Commander of ye said Ship ye Coronation, or any of the officers belonging to ye same".

The exact site of the wreck of Coronation on the seabed off Penlee Point was to remain undiscovered for 275 years. But in 1967, a group of Plymouth amateur divers, Terry Harrison, Alan Down and George Sandford while diving there suddenly spotted some cannonballs and then some more! That trail led them along until they were quite close in near Penlee Point. And in shallow water they were surrounded by cannon. They kept the position of the cannon to themselves until they were able to contact Alan Bax of SNAP and in April 1968 were able to lead him to the site and show him the cannon. Alan Bax's early surveys of the site showed that there were 40 cannon among the rocks close in and there, too, were bronze pulley wheels bearing the Navy's broad arrow mark. This made it almost certain that they had found Coronation.

Year after year careful exploration of the site confirmed that they had a man o'war of the right date, but it was left to archaeologist Peter McBride to confirm it. He carried out a magnetomer search in 1977 and found another site for the ship, half a mile from the Penlee cannon and in 20m of water. In this place he found 14 iron cannon and most important of all a pewter plate which bore the arms of the Skelton family.

There now seems little doubt that Coronation broke in half, or broke up where the 40 cannons lie and drifted on to the site found by Peter McBride. Though diving is forbidden without permission on both sites, divers anywhere in that part of the Sound should keep their eyes open for other cannon. So far only 54 have been found!

Vectis. Collier.
Sunk: February 15,1912. Possible loss of rudder.
Position: Andurn Point.
Depth: 9m.

This 907-ton steamer was wrecked on her return run to Cardiff after unloading a cargo of coal in the Cattewater. After passing the western end of the Breakwater, the steamer suddenly altered course and steamed at full speed on to the rocks of Andurn Point. She was stuck there until the Christmas hurricane at the end of the year broke her into small pieces. The shattered wreckage is to be found over a wide area around the Point in under 10m.

Tinker Shoal.
Depth: 20m.

A good drift-dive over a broken reef in 20m. During the course of such a dive you will pass over a great deal of small wreckage.

Nepaul. P and O liner
Sunk: December 10, 1890. Bad navigation.
Position: 50 19 02N; 04 07 28.
Depth: 10m.

A 375 foot-long ship of 3550 tons, she was homeward bound from Calcutta for London when she ran on to the Shagstone in the dark. She had landed most of her passengers at Marseilles and the small number that were still aboard were taken off by one of the Plymouth pilot boats.

It was hoped to refloat her on the next high tide, but when the tide came back, all it did was to fill her up inside. Her bottom had been badly ripped open. She became a total loss and is now very broken Her wreckage is mixed with that of the trawler Baroda which thought she was safe following in the liner's wake and was much surprised to find herself wrecked less than 100 yards from the Nepaul.

It is difficult to tell which wreckage is which, particularly as the steamer Constance is there too. It is safe to say that the big winches and big anchor are the Nepaul's, as are most of the steel plates and ribs which lie amid kelp in less than10m. There is a good deal of broken pottery in the area, but unless you find some with the P and O crest, it could belong to any one of the three.

Nepaul, which hit the Shagstone in the dark

Constance. British merchant steamer.
Sunk: January 21,1888. Lost in fog.
Position: 50 19 02N; 04 07 28W.
Depth:13m

This British steamer of 850 tons was on passage from Antwerp to Plymouth, when she ran into the Shagstone in fog. The 209ft ship was carrying a cargo of hides and she now lies, very broken just south-east of the Shagstone. Three of the crew were killed when they were thrown out of the lifeboat when abandoning ship in heavy seas.

Glen Strathallan. Millionaire's yacht.
Sunk: April 27, 1970. Scuttled deliberately.
Position: 50 18 56N; 04 07 37W.
Depth: 14m.

Once a trawler, then a millionaire's plaything, then a training ship and finally the first and only ship in Britain to be sunk specially for divers. She lies to the south of the Shagstone and is very broken.

The Glen Strathallan was built as a 330-ton trawler in 1928, 150ft long with a beam of 22ft and was then converted by Mr Colby Cubbin, a multi-millionaire, for £30,000 into a pleasure yacht.

In World War Two the Glen Strathallan went to war with the Navy as an escort ship. At the end of the war Mr Cubbin got his yacht back and used it for cruising until his death. In his will he stipulated that she should be used as a training ship for boys – and for years she was – and that when too old for that, the ship should be sunk in deep water. Which is how it happened that she was scuttled in her present position as an underwater classroom for divers training at Fort Bovisand. Not deep enough though; the wreck had to be dispersed a year later. The bows are still recognisable and her big boiler stands clear in a sand patch. Otherwise the wreckage has a heavy kelp covering.

HMS Elk. Trawler-danlayer.
Sunk: November 27, 1940. Hit a mine.
Position: 50 18 24 N; 04 10 12W.
Depth: 27m.

This 181-ton Grimsby fishing trawler was built in 1902. In 1915 she was hired by the Navy as a minesweeper and served until 1919, when she returned to fishing. In 1939, she was called up again and used as a danlayer.

When she struck the mine, she took some time to sink and all aboard were saved. In 1981 she was found by amateur divers lying upright without her superstructure on a sand bottom and since then has been heavily dived. She is 5m proud of a seabed at 27m. The port side shows more damage than the other. She is 108ft long. The bows are complete with winch. A hole opens entry to the engine room, but much of the plating is rusting and there are some very sharp edges. Lobsters are under some broken off plates. There are large congers inside her.

She has been totally stripped of all removeable items with the portholes and the telegraph going first. Her anchor has been raised. Outside the Elk in 34m there is a sudden drop-off of 10m down to 44m. This steep bank may be the sign of a former coastline of millions of years ago. The bank is covered with gorgonias.

Moments after this picture was taken, this millionaire's yacht was scuttled.

HMS Foyle. Destroyer-torpedo boat
Sunk: March 15, 1917. Under tow after mined.
Position: 50 16 42N; 04 10 48W.
Depth: 46m.

There is a story that the Foyle was mined in the Dover Straits on March 15, 1917, when 27 Navy men were killed out of her crew of 70. The story says her bow was blown right off and sank, but the stern section stayed afloat and was taken in tow for Plymouth for a new bow to be fitted. The stern section is said to have sunk before reaching the Sound. These stories about the sinking of HMS Foyle are completely inaccurate.

Some official records do have her listed as mined in the Dover Straits, but her captain, Lieutenant A.H.D.Young, RNR., would violently disagree. His report of the sinking (now in the Public Record Office at Kew) says that he was patrolling the eastern area off the Devon coast in the early hours of March 15, 1917, and when the Foyle was just over three miles to the east of the Eddystone Rocks, she struck a mine.

The explosion was enormous, and not only ripped out the bottom of the ship on the port side, but also destroyed some of the mess decks, killing 27 men in their bunks and leaving two others critically injured.

Immediate checks showed that she was taking in water rapidly in two of her boiler rooms. Watertight doors were closed and some of the bulkheads shored up to try and prevent them from collapsing. Three men were found to be trapped by twisted metal and a party led by the First Officer went to their assistance. Two of these men were released though they were badly injured. The third man, however, couldn't be freed, though he was still alive.

A passing steamer was signalled and at about 8.30 a.m. the collier John O'Scott came alongside to help. All the injured and most of the crew were transferred to the steamer which then took Foyle in tow by the stern. By towing her stern first it was hoped that the twisted plates holding the trapped man would give enough to enable him to be released.

By this time, both HMS Boyne and HMS Bittern were alongside and sent men over with tools to free the man. They suceeded, but only at the cost of amputating his right leg..

The towing hawser was transferred to the tug Illustrious and she began to pull Foyle towards Plymouth. However, at 2.10 p.m. she began to settle by the head. Her captain gave this position as Rame Head bearing North 39 degrees west, the Breakwater Light bearing North 21 degrees east and the Mewstone bearing North 75 degrees east.

Mined near the Eddystone, not the Dover Straits.

That report has the ring of truth about it. The wreck is definitely that of the Foyle as divers recovered her nameplate in 1972.

The wreck is on a sandy bed at 46m and mostly only a metre or two proud, though one or two pieces stand up 6m. Her big boilers are clear. Her starboard side is collapsing inwards. As she is now very broken and it is easy to stir up the silt on her, it is difficult to orientate yourself, especially as diving reports say that she is sinking into the seabed. However, the viz can be as much as 10m. HMS Foyle was built by Cammell Laird in 1903. The 550 ton ship was 225ft long with a beam of 23.5ft, and had 7 000 hp engines which would give her over 25 knots. She had one 12-pounder gun, five 6-pounders, and two 18-inch torpedo tubes, but only one gun shows now. The others may be under the great pile of wreckage towards her bow. The torpedo tubes are easy to see.

WARNING: This wreck may be listed under the Military Remains Act as a war grave (see Dive Planning).

Stanhope. British steamer.
Sunk: June 17, 1917. Torpedoed.
Position: 50 11 09N; 04 08 21W
Depth: 58m.

On June 15, 1917, UB-31, commanded by Oberleutnant Bieber, torpedoed the Teesdale, but her captain managed to beach her. Bieber went on hunting. On June 17, he found the 2854-ton Stanhope and shadowed her for a while before firing a torpedo from periscope depth. The 333ft British steamer went down like a stone and 22 of her crew were lost, though her captain survived. She had been heading for Dunkirk from Barrow with a cargo of steel rails.

This ship, which was built by Ropner and Sons in 1900 for the English Steamship Company, now lies broken in two amidships Depth is 58m to the seabed and 47m to her deck. . She is on a slope with the southern end the shallowest part.

Claverley. Steam Collier.
Sunk: August 20, 1917. Torpedoed.
Position: 50 08 37N; 04 10 21W.
Depth: 62m.

At 2 a.m. Claverley was making her maximum speed of 8 knots down Channel, bound from the Tyne to Genoa with 5,700 tons of coal. The night was clear and the wind a light south-westerly. The Master, Hugh Jones, was in his bunk and had left instructions to be woken when the ship was off the Eddystone.

As he slept, Oberleutnant Umberger manoeuvered his boat, UB-38, so that her bow was pointing directly at the dark shape of the 3829-ton British steamer, which was crossing right in front of the surfaced submarine.

At that moment the Mate sent one of the 58 crewmen aboard to wake the Master, but he hadn't quite reached the captain's cabin when Umberger's torpedo struck the ship's port side.

Ten men died in the explosion. The Master who had been thrown from his bunk by the blast ordered "Abandon ship" as soon as he reached the deck. All the crew crammed into the only undamaged boat and pulled clear as the 350ft steamer started to turn turtle.

The survivors reported later that they saw two submarines on the surface near their upside down ship, and that they were questioned from the conning-tower of the smaller of the two U-boats about their cargo and destination. Both submarines soon dived.

At 9.45 a.m. an airship from Plymouth hovered over the wreck and then HMT No.125, the Agnes Wickfield, arrived and took the survivors aboard. As the Claverley showed no sign of sinking, the Agnes Wickfield was instructed by radio to sink her. Eight shells into the hull sent her down.

Today the steamer, built in 1907 by W. Doxford and Sons of Sunderland, is described by Plymouth Sound divers as "big and upright". She is on a flat sand-mud seabed at 62m from which she stands 7m proud. Her 4.7-inch stern gun is still in place.

Brigitte. Armed Steamer.
Sunk: November 19, 1942. Torpedoed by E-boat.
Position: 50 08 11N; 04 09 11W.
Depth: 64m.

In convoy on November 19, 1942, this 1595-ton British steamer, bound for Barry from Southampton in ballast, was the centre of two E-boat attacks during the dark early hours. In addition to her crew she carried two Naval gunners and the Convoy Commodore and his staff, making 23 on board in all.

The first attack on the convoy came shortly after 3am when they were crossing Bigbury Bay. Enemy aircraft attacked first, and then, to add to the confusion, in came the E-boats from a flotilla based at Cherbourg. The Yewforest, another ship in the convoy, was sunk, but then the E-boats withdrew and the convoy steamed on down Channel.

Six miles further on, the E-boats attacked again. This time it was the Brigitte which took a torpedo in her port side. Seven crew, the two gunners and one of the Convoy Commodore's staff were lost.

The ship is still intact on a black mud seabed at 64m. Her highest point is her bridge at 51m.

Lab. Norwegian steamer.
Sunk: November 18, 1942. Torpedoed.
Position: 50 07 39N; 04 10 09W.
Depth: 63m.

This 1118-ton steamer, 226ft long with a crew of 21, was on her way for Mumbles from Southampton in ballast on November 18, 1942 when an E-boat torpedoed her in the dark. Three of the crew were lost when she sank. Plymouth Sound divers describe her as very broken up and in several pieces and only 5m off the flat sand-mud seabed at 63m.

Section FOUR.

Diving Sites to the East of the Sound.

Admiralty Charts:
1613 (Eddystone Rocks to Berry Head)
1900 (Approaches to Plymouth)
1267 (Falmouth to Plymouth)

Divers are asked to look, but not touch in this voluntary marine reserve.

Great Mewstone.
Depths: To 30m on south side.

This rocky island, with its remarkable steep shelving face, is 59m high. The Little Mewstone, which is 15m high, sits on the middle of the Mewstone Ledge, which runs out 400yds to the south-west of the Great Mewstone.

Though the Mewstone is now uninhabited and belongs to the Ministry of Defence, people have lived on it. In 1774, a local Plymouth man, guilty only of some minor crime, was sentenced to be "transported" to the island for a term of seven years. The man lived there with his family and completed his sentence without once setting foot on the mainland. When the sentence was up, the family moved off the island. The daughter, known as "Black Joan", opted to stay. She married and raised three children on the Mewstone until her husband fell from one of the steep rocks and was drowned.

In the early 1800's Sam Wakeman and his wife Ann, lived there in a hut – now in ruins – with a garden, chickens and pigs. He lived rent free in return for protecting the island's rabbits for Mr Charles Calmady, the owner, to shoot. Wakeman later gave up the island and became a boatman at the Barbican steps. In the late 1920's the island changed hands for £575.

It is certain that at one time it was possible to wade out to the Mewstone at low tide. Not always successfully, judging by this entry in the Wembury Church Register – "Burials, 1720. May 15. Richard Cragg, Robert Sampson, Mary Avent, Mary Hake, John Tingcomb, 17, Josias Avent, 21, Walter Avent, 29, Mary Beer, 30, Elizabeth Taylor. Drowned between the Mew Stone and the Continent on a Sunday."

The Mewstones and the Ledge have claimed many ships. An extraordinary number of sailing ship captains seemed to think it easy to sail between the Mewstone and the shore, but that narrow passage is only 50yds wide and the rocks running out from the shore to Culter Rock or north from the Mewstone itself proved the opposite.

There are plenty of wrecks for divers to look out for. For example, the Norwegian barque **August Smith** was wrecked on Wembury Beach in 1895. In 1897, the brigantine **St Pierre,** of Le Havre, en route for Madagascar and loaded with coal briquettes, struck the Mewstone and foundered. Divers have found some of her cargo.

Earlier victims were the smack **Industry** in 1851, and a year later the 206 ton brig **Ocean Queen** went down on the Little Mewstone with the loss of all but one of her 15-man crew.

Ajax. Paddlesteamer.
Sunk: October 13, 1854. "Sheer negligence".
Position: Little Mewstone.
Depth: 12m.

A regular service between London and Cork, calling at Plymouth on the way, was operated by this 800-ton London-registered paddlesteamer On October 12, 1854 she left London with 350 passengers and, in her 206ft hull, carried general cargo, chests of tea and tons of guano for use as fertiliser. Her captain, Rochford, was standing in for the regular captain, who was ill. On October 13, Ajax was approaching Plymouth – much too close in. The captain rejected the advice of Chief Officer Steel, to give the Mewstone a wider berth, and held his course.

It was flat calm and visibility was perfect. Even so the Ajax ran straight on to the Little Mewstone and ripped her bottom open on the Mewstone Ledge. Despite panic among the passengers, all were safely taken off by boats out of Plymouth. The Ajax became a total wreck.

A contemporary coastguard report recorded that the wreck was "either done purposely or else from sheer culpable negligence". Captain Rochford had lost another steamer, the Minerva only two months earlier on the Skerries near Holyhead!

There is plenty of wreckage to be found on the site in 12m of water just to the South of the Little Mewstone, though some of this wreckage may be that of the Rothesay or the Matilda. In the gullies amid the kelp are decking and winches, with one piece sticking up above the kelp to a height of over 3m.

Matilda. Fishing vessel
Sunk: March 1, 1866. Careless navigation.
Position: On top of Ajax.
Depth: 12m

Matilda was a casualty of the engines of the Ajax on to which she ran when passing the Mewstone on her way back to Plymouth. She sank so swiftly that only William Bunce, a boy, survived from her crew of three.

Rothesay. Steam coaster.
Sunk: October 15, 1877. Storm winds.
Position: On top of Ajax
Depth: 12m

This 332-ton steamer was in ballast heading home

for Cardiff from Caen when she was caught in near hurricane winds and decided to run for shelter of Plymouth. Just before midnight the Rothesay was blown on to the rocks surrounding the Mewstones. When she struck one of the crew was washed overboard and carried unhurt on to the Great Mewstone. With his help the crew left on board the Rothesay managed to get a line to shore and escaped along it as the ship began to break up.

In the daylight at Low the Rothesay presented an amazing sight – a dozen holes could be seen in her hull and both stem and stern posts had been torn completely off.

The wreckage of the Rothesay is mixed with that of the Ajax and is also spread over a wide area in gullies in shallow water amid the kelp.

Nillus Cannon Wreck.
Sunk: In 18th century. Reason not known.
Position: South side of Great Mewstone.
Depth: 10m

The south side of the Great Mewstone leading out to the Ledge, is all steep-sided gullies and mounds and over a dozen iron cannon lie among them amid heavy kelp growth. The site was discovered by Dick Middlewood of Croydon BSAC in 1968. Two huge anchors – one nearly 10ft long – and much broken pottery were found later in a combined survey of the site by the Croydon divers and Slough Sub-Aqua Club. Dating the cannon, the anchors, and the red pottery, possibly from Spanish oil jars, point to a ship of the middle or late 18th century. Divers from Chester Sub-Aqua Club found a ship's bell in the area which could be 17th or 18th century. It bore just one word "Nillus". The Ajax wreckage encroaches on this site.

The Mewstone Drop-off.
Depth: 40m.

To the south, the gullies follow the run of the steep face of the Great Mewstone going down and out. They drop down swiftly to 30m. Here there is some evidence of an aircraft wreck and in 1984 diver David Swales and the author found part of a very corroded belt of 0.5in tracer bullets, similar to those used in Flying Fortresses. From the bottom of the gullies in 30m there is a sudden cliff face falling sheer to 40m.

"Mewstone Submarine". "German U-boat"
Sunk: Not known
Position: 50 18 12N; 04 06 30W
Depth: 26m

The 1984 report of a World War One U-boat jammed into a gully of the Little Mewstone was probably a hoax. But if so, it was an elaborate one. A position - 50 18 12; 04 06 30 - was given, placing her about 100 yards south of the Little Mewstone. She was said to be about 100 feet long, lying at an angle of 45 degrees in the gully, which runs down from the sub's bow in 12m to her stern in 26m. There were no periscopes to be seen and no propellor though the boss was said to be still there. She was described as about 12ft high and it was also said that divers had been inside her, though this had entailed taking off their gear to enter the hatch.

Plymouth diving experts expressed grave doubts about her existence soon after publication of the report. And still do so. Another diver more recently reported a great length of piping in the same area, which sounds more likely.

The Astrolabe.
Sunk: 17th century (or lost overboard).
Position: Gully to north-west of Great Mewstone.
Depth: 11m.

The waters inside the Great Mewstone are sheltered and ideal for training dives. The depth is rarely more

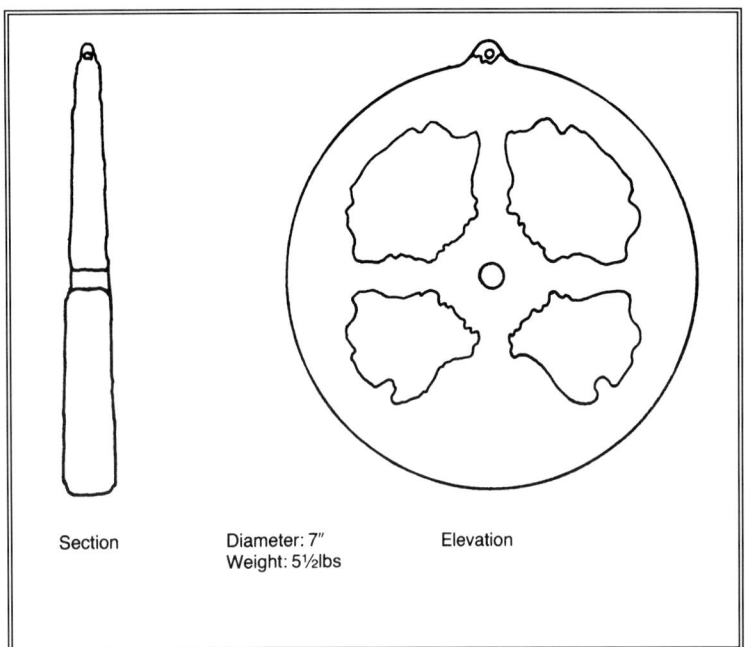

The astrolabe found by Wilf Jenkins - only the 32nd in the world.

than 11m, with sand patches leading to gullies which run north-west into the face of the Mewstone reef. The floor of these is coarse sand and shingle and the gullies are roofed with kelp. An extra-ordinary find was made here by Wilf Jenkin of Plymouth Sound BSAC in September 1970. Among the sea-growth in one gully he found a bronze astrolabe, one of the early instruments used in navigation. His discovery of this ring of brass was only the 32nd astrolabe known to exist in the world today. Experts dated the Mewstone find to the first quarter of the 17th century and said that it was probably English.

If there was a navigation instrument, where is the wreck? A good question, but despite extensive searches of thousands of square yards by Plymouth Sound BSAC, nothing else has been found.

Cannonball Gully.
Position: 50 18 30N; 04 06 52W
Depth: 9m.
North of the Great Mewstone is a gully with heavily concreted cannonballs in it.
WARNING: Do not dive if red flags are flying from HMS Cambridge Gunnery School.

Black Stone Reef.
Depth: 18m
This area of rough ground starts 800yds south-west of Blackstone Point near the entrance to the River Yealm, and rises to within 3m of the surface. A very pretty area of good diving ground, it consists of rocks, some six or seven metres high, with many gullies to 18m. Fish life is very plentiful and deadmen's fingers, jewel anemones, and soft corals provide the background. This is a big area at least 100yds square and it can be spotted easily by the tidal turbulance over it.

Hilsea Point Rocks.
Depth: 26m
Some Plymouth divers say this is the best scenic dive in this part of Devon. The rocks are 800yds south-east of Hilsea Point and almost directly south of the old coastguard lookout which is a quarter-mile east of the Point itself, 90m high on the cliffs. The rocks are really pinnacles, seven or eight of them, the tallest of which rises to within 2m of the surface from the seabed at 24-26m.

Rocks and sand are between the pinnacles, one of which has a hole in it which divers can swim through. These tall and slender pinnacles are a wonderful sight in good vis with hard corals, soft corals, sea fans, and big sea urchins decorating them, and clouds of fish surrounding them, parting to let big ling swim through. Some very old wreckage lies at the foot of the largest of the pinnacles.

Drawback is the fierce tide which runs here and which reaches one-and-a-half knots at times. Diving must be done on slack or after half tide which means three hours before high or three hours 20 minutes after high.

The West Rutts.
Depth: 36m.

Four miles west of the East Rutts. Between the two Rutts and to the south of them is a strange area of sand waves, some with crests 5m high. The "run" of the waves is north-south with 100-300yds between the crests. The rocks of the West Rutts are not so dramatic as those of East Rutts, rising only from 36m to 25m. Most of the ground is rough with gravel and sand patches among the rocks. There are some large rocks with crab and lobster and crawfish in season, but these Rutts are not as good a dive as the eastern version.

Australbush. Armed steamer.
Sunk: November 13,1917. Torpedoed.
Position: 50 12 12N; 04 05 15
Depth: 56m.

The 4398-ton Australbush was armed with a 6-pounder Australian-made gun and carried two Australian Navy gunners to handle it. She was part of a convoy that left Le Havre on November 12,1917, with most ships bound for Barry Roads in ballast. All went well until the next day when she had lost the convoy and had to travel on her own.

At 1.40 p.m. when the Master, James Duncan, was in the chartroom, the second mate sighted the white wake of a torpedo only 200 yards away. The torpedo, fired by UC-31, struck the port side at No.3 hold. The force of the explosion not only ripped a hole in the port side, but badly damaged the starboard side too. The ship began to sink rapidly by the stern seven miles north-east of the Eddystone.

As the boats got clear of the ship, the third engineer and a seaman didn't leave go of a line from the davits quickly enough and an upward surge of the ship wrench them out of the boat. At that moment the ship sank. Both men disappeared with her. Two Admiralty trawlers picked other survivors up and landed them at Plymouth.

Depth to the top of the wreck is 44m and 56m to the seabed. She is known locally as "The Coal Boat" and lies north-south. She has been trawled into many times and there are nets on her.

Lord Stonehaven. Naval trawler.
Sunk: October 2,1942. By German E-boat.
Position: 50 11 43N; 04 05 31W.
Depth: 58m.

Though listed by the Admiralty as an "unknown", Plymouth Sound divers are certain that this trawler sitting upright on the bottom is the Lord Stonehaven, **an Admiralty requisitioned trawler which was sunk by E-boats during an attack on a convoy off the Eddystone on October 2, 1942.** The 444-ton craft, which was built in 1934, is intact. All the shellcases, and small arms cartridges and her batteries are dated no later than 1941.

WARNING: This wreck is netted with both tangle and gill nets.

"Eastern Coal Boat". Probably collier.
Sunk: Not known
Position: 50 10 21N; 04 03 01
Depth: 59m.

Local fishermen call her "The Eastern Coal Boat". She is a small steamer only 52ft long. She lies east-west and is very broken. She has been trawled into many times and coal in the trawls gave her that name - so watch out for nets. She is 6m proud of a sand-mud seabed at 59m.

Visborg. Steam Collier.
Sunk: November 27, 1916. Bombs planted by U-boat.
Position: 50 05 32N; 04 06 03W.
Depth: 68m.

This Norwegian steamer of 1311 tons is interesting as she was one of the last victims of Oberleutnant Erich Noodt in UB-19 just three days before he was sunk in a famous action by the Q-ship Penshurst.

The 245ft Visborg was laden with 1760 tons of coal from Barry and heading for Cherbourg when she was stopped by Noodt, who planted bombs which sent her to the bottom. All the crew were saved.

UB-19 motored on and the same day sank the Belle Ile of 1884 tons, a Norwegian steamer carrying iron ore from Spain to France. On November 30, Erich Noodt was lured within range by the 1191-ton Q-ship Penshurst – with her low freeboard and funnel aft looking very much like an oil tanker – by the simple device of stopping and all the crew apparently abandoning ship.

When the unsuspecting U-boat came within 250yds on the surface, the Navy gun crews left aboard pumped shells from both their hidden three-pounders and 12-pounder into the sub. They hit her with over 80 rounds and the 118ft U-boat sank bow first. Noodt and thirteen of his crew were captured, seven died. Captain F.H. Grenfell and the crew of the Penshurst sank another submarine on January 14, 1917, the UB-37, commanded by Oberleutnant P. Gunther.

The Visborg, though too deep for most divers in 68m, is intact and stands 13m proud.

Persier. Belgian Relief Steamer.
Sunk: February 11, 1945. Torpedoed.
Position: 50 17 00N; 03 58 09W.
Depth: 28m.

The Persier never completed her mercy mission. Oberleutnant Werner Riecken and his crew of 34 in UB-1017 saw to that. But though he torpedoed her, he didn't see her sink – and nor did anyone else. It was not until Plymouth Sound BSAC found her in May, 1969, that anyone knew where she was.

The story of the Persier's last voyage begins on February 8, 1945. She left Cardiff on a mercy mission – to take food to the liberated but starving people of Belgium. There were 63 people on board the ship when she sailed, some of them survivors of the Leopoldville, which, torpedoed, sank off Cherbourg on Christmas night, 1944. These survivors had asked to be repatriated and as the Persier was the first ship to head for a Belgian port, they were put aboard. For this voyage the 5382-ton Belgian steamer, which had originally been called the War Buffalo when she was launched at Newcastle in 1918, was to be part of Convoy No. BTC 65. The convoy commander, Commodore Edmund Wood and his staff of three signallers were aboard.

On February 11, the convoy was between the Eddystone and the shore when Commodore Wood received a message from one of the small escorts that a periscope had been seen. Not long afterwards a column of water shot skywards on the port side of the convoy. Older hands guessed that it was the premature explosion of a German torpedo. They were right. Within seconds another torpedo hissed past the stern of the Persier from port to starboard and disappeared. On the bridge Captain Mathieu, First Officer Lardinoy and Commodore Wood braced themselves. They knew what was coming and at 5.25pm precisely, it did. The torpedo struck the port side opposite No.2 hold and just forward of the

They saw her torpedoed, but no one saw her sink. Found years later by divers, the Persier is now dived regularly from Bovisand.

bridge. The explosion flung Lardinoy to the deck and broke his nose. On board UB-1017 the crew believed they had hit two ships – the premature explosion of the earlier torpedo, they thought, was another hit. Riecken later reported two ships sunk.

On board Persier, as the sea poured into the damaged hold, the boxes of powdered egg, tins of baby food and meat, broke loose and five tons of woollen blankets soaked up the sea. The ship started to list to port. Abandon ship drill took only six minutes, but it went terribly wrong. Lifeboat No.1, with Commodore Wood and ten others, was launched correctly, but the enormous seas unhooked the bow and left it suspended by the stern, spilling everyone into the water. Lifeboat No.3 was drawn into the ship's still-spinning propellor and was chopped to pieces. Lifeboat No.1 was then righted, but as three men slid down the falls to her, one, a stoker, caught his foot and was left hanging, smashed against the side of the ship by every wave. The two other men fared little better reaching the boat safely, but it was then also drawn into the propeller.

The ship was now about four miles from the Eddystone in winds of Force 7. The seas were colossal, but rafts were launched and men managed to cling to them. The Persier was not moving, with her propeller stopped. But she was obviously not long for the surface. Her stern was right out of the water. Still aboard were her captain, Lardinoy, and five others. It was then that Lardinoy put forward a desperate idea. He would swim to a nearby small cargo ship, the Birker Force and ask the captain to come alongside and rescue them. To get him away from the ship, he asked the other men to throw him as far out as they could. That is exactly what they did.

Lardinoy, despite being thumped by nearby depth-charging, managed to swim to a lifeboat which had been launched from the Birker Force and gasped out his message. As the ship moved in on the Persier, the last men on board flung an old unseaworthy raft into the sea and jumped for it. They were all picked up. In all, 44 were saved out of the Persier's complement of 63. Persier was last seen drifting into the night, stern high, bow down. Tugs sent out from Plymouth searched in vain.

She sank in the dark and no one saw her going. And no one would know where she was today if Colin Hopkins, chairman then of Plymouth Sound BSAC, after being told by a sea-angling friend of a place he was always losing tackle, dived the site and found the wreck of a large armed merchantman with a 4.7in gun on her stern and two sets of Oerlikon guns, one on the stern and one on the bridge. She had a bronze propellor.

Plymouth Sound BSAC confirmed her name when they recovered her bell – still clearly marked War Buffalo. They bought the Persier for £300 and 12 members of the branch put up the money.

The Persier today is right off the mouth of the Erme with her bows to the south-west. Her bow is her highest point about 10m above the seabed at 28m. She is over on her port side and very broken amidships, where she is lying over rock outcrops. Her centre has collapsed inwards. The three boilers are clear to see. Nearby is an 8ft anchor. Her propellor and three guns have all been salvaged.

Diver-cox'ns should approach from the east, the Burgh Island side, then drag anchor or grapnel until hooked in. Try the same tactic from the west and you will certainly only hook into the big reef before the wreckage.

Marks: North-south: Open up the bluff at the mouth of the Erme until you can see the old coastguard cottages. Line up on the first chimney. East-west mark: On the sky-line near Thurlestone there is a big Christmas-tree shaped tree. Put this slightly to the right of the fork between the main two peaks on Burgh Island.

The Other Persier: She may be at 50 17 00; 03 58 22. In May, 1980, a diver reported that he had missed the wreck of the Persier and had found himself on another wreck – that of a steel vessel complete with portholes, and two boilers 20ft high, all on a reef some 2m high off a seabed at 25m. He estimated that he was about 380m east-south-east of the real wreck of the Persier. This might have been thought to be part of the Persier and local dive boat skippers searched the area in vain. However, completely independently, Jim Gill of Bovisand has also reported being on a wreck that "was clearly not the Persier" with a bow section standing well proud. His report of the "Other Persier" however put the new wreck some 500m south of the Persier.

Maine. Cargo Steamer.
Sunk: March 23, 1917. Torpedoed.
Position: 50 12 45N; 03 50 53W.
Depth: 37m.

She was a dirty British cargo-ship with a salt-caked smoke-stack and she came zigzagging down the Channel on a mad March day in 1917. Watching her through the periscope of his U-boat, UC-17, was Oberleutnant Ralph Wenninger. Rain squalls stopped anyone aboard the 3616-ton Maine spotting him and on Friday, March 23, at 8.05am, his torpedo struck her full in the port side, level with No. 2 hold. The blast knocked Captain "Bill" Johnston off his feet,

The Maine was a victim of UC-17.

blew off the hatches of No. 2 and No. 3 holds, smashed the port gig and wrecked the bridge. And it made a great hole in her side through which water poured on to her cargo of chalk, horsehair and goatskins. Captain Johnston felt her settling by the head and sent off distress calls, before heading for the land.

First help to arrive was a Royal Navy torpedo boat, No. 99, captained by Lieutenant-Commander Percy Taylor of the R.N.R. He had been in command of a flotilla of minesweepers, busy clearing mines from the entrances to Dartmouth and Teignmouth – some of which had been laid by Wenninger and UC-17 – and had been on his way home to Devonport.

Taylor put his ship alongside the Maine and took off most of the crew. Captain Johnston had told him that his ship was now completely out of action with the midships fully flooded, but the Commander thought there might be a chance of beaching her in Bigbury Bay, probably Hope Cove, and so passed a towline to the stricken ship. Other patrol boats now arrived and helped with the tow too, but progress was very slow. At noon the first tug arrived and took over the tow. It was too late. Soon after the new tow was established, the Maine's internal bulkheads collapsed and at 12.45pm she sank. She did so in Commander Taylor's words: "Gracefully, upright and on an even keel". By then Oberleutnant Wenninger had taken his submarine away to the north-east, heading homeward for Zeebrugge, base of the Flanders Flotilla.

For a long time the Maine's position was quite clear. Her two masts stuck up 12 feet clear of the surface and the Admiralty issued a Notice to Mariners about this hazard. (See next page).

In time both her masts collapsed and, for some reason known only to themselves, the local fishermen called her "the Railway Line Wreck" (could it be some dreadful joke about Maine Line?).

She was first dived in 1961 by Torbay BSAC, who bought her for £100 and salvaged her bronze prop for which they received £840. Then the gun was salvaged off her stern. And in 1983 another diving team from

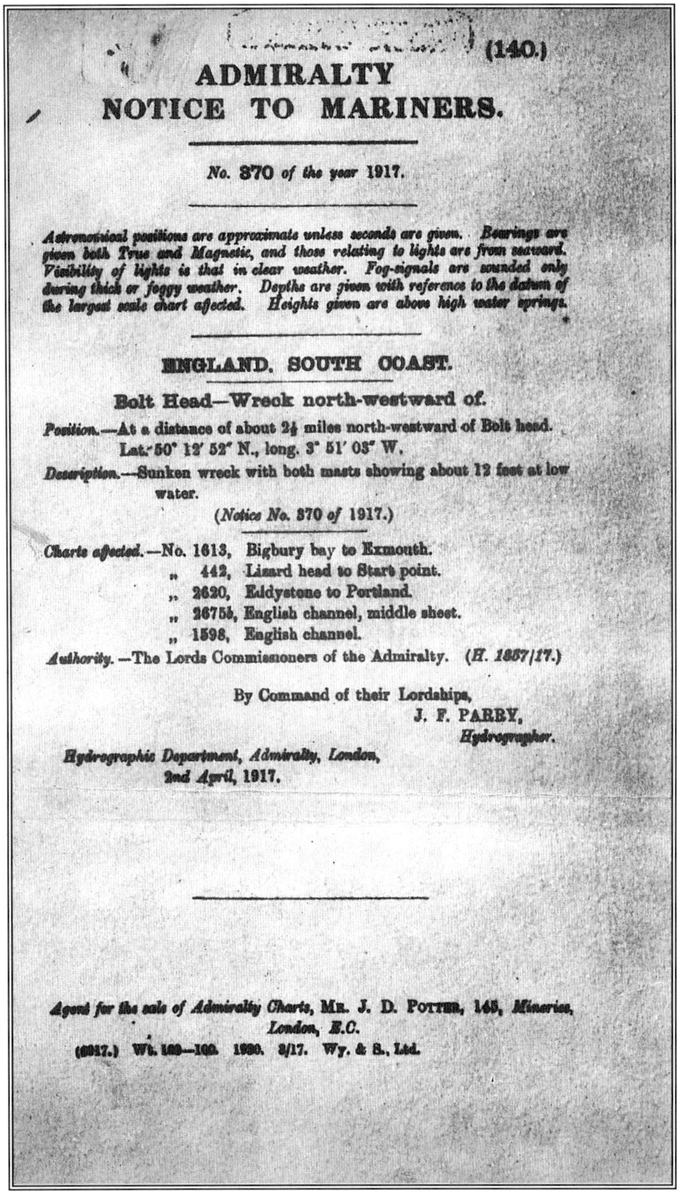

(140.)

ADMIRALTY
NOTICE TO MARINERS.

No. 370 of the year 1917.

Astronomical positions are approximate unless seconds are given. Bearings are given both True and Magnetic, and those relating to lights are from seaward. Visibility of lights is that in clear weather. Fog-signals are sounded only during thick or foggy weather. Depths are given with reference to the datum of the largest scale chart affected. Heights given are above high water springs.

ENGLAND, SOUTH COAST.

Bolt Head—Wreck north-westward of.

Position.—At a distance of about 2¼ miles north-westward of Bolt head.
Lat. 50° 12′ 52″ N., long. 3° 51′ 03″ W.

Description.—Sunken wreck with both masts showing about 12 feet at low water.

(*Notice No. 370 of 1917.*)

Charts affected.—No. 1613, Bigbury bay to Exmouth.
„ 442, Lizard head to Start point.
„ 2620, Eddystone to Portland.
„ 2675b, English channel, middle sheet.
„ 1598, English channel.

Authority.—The Lords Commissioners of the Admiralty. (*H. 1867/17.*)

By Command of their Lordships,
J. F. PARRY,
Hydrographer.

Hydrographic Department, Admiralty, London,
2nd April, 1917.

Agent for the sale of Admiralty Charts, MR. J. D. POTTER, 145, *Minories, London, E.C.*
(6017.) Wt. 189—109. 1930. 3/17. Wy. & S., Ltd.

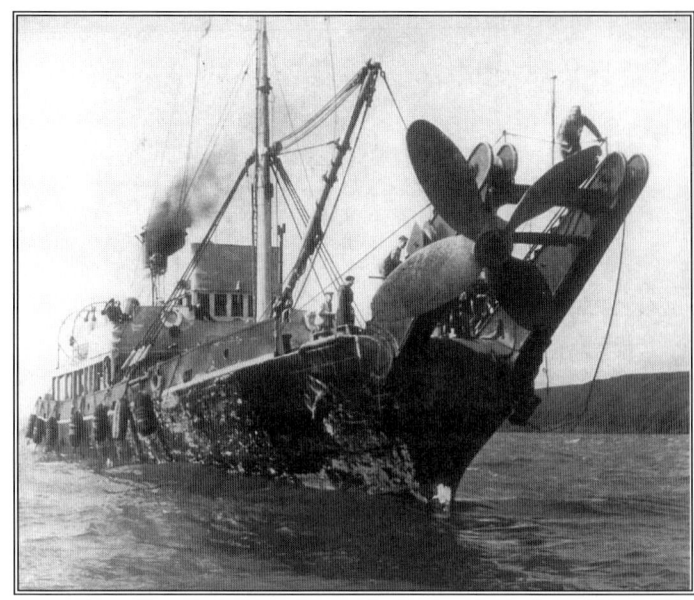

The raising of the Maine's propellor in 1961 by Torbay BS-AC needed a little help from the Admiralty ship Barbastel.

Torbay BSAC raised the spare iron propellor from her deck. It is now on display at the front of the Victoria Shopping Centre, Paignton.

Wenninger did not escape scot free. He was sunk by a mine when going through the Dover Barrage on April 22, 1918. He and 20 of his men made a free ascent from the crippled submarine in 30m. Only six survived, one of whom was Wenninger. He spent the rest of the war in a British prison camp for officers at Donnington Hall, Leicestershire, and when last heard of in 1929, was the executive officer of the German cruiser Berlin.

The Maine today is one of the most popular dives in Devon, probably because she is easily accessible and is still a very ship-like ship. She is , upright on an even keel on a shingle seabed at 37m from which she is 15m proud. Though both her props and the gun have been salvaged, divers should remember she does belong to Torbay Branch and, though they don't

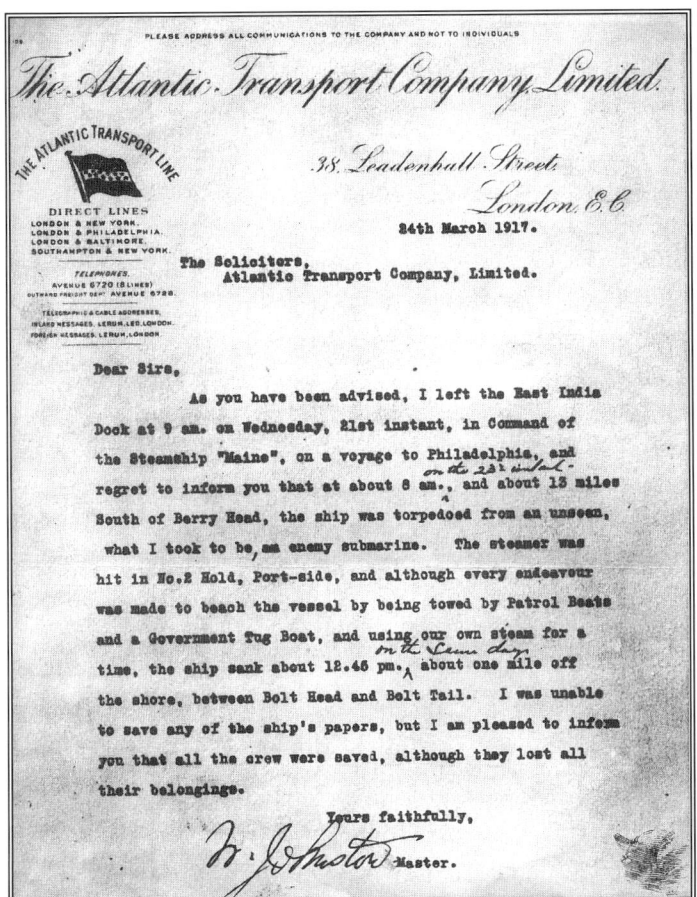

As soon as he was safely back on land, Captain Johnston wrote this letter to the Maine's owners.

was in the bottom of a hole near the big deck anchor winches and only the tip of the tang was showing. The two divers presented the bell to the Maine's owners, Torbay BS-AC.

The Maine was built for the Sierra Shipping Co of Liverpool and was called Sierra Blanca when launched in 1905. She was 375ft overall, 361ft between perpendiculars as she had an overhanging counter stern of 14 feet. Her beam is 46.2ft. She was renamed in 1913 by the Atlantic Transport Co.

The Maine was soon carrying war cargoes and was nearly destroyed by one of them when she caught fire on October 26, 1915, in Boulogne Docks while packed with cases of explosives. Lieutenant-Commander Arthur Warden went into her holds and put the fire out with a fire hose. He was presented with an Albert Medal by King George V for his "special gallantry" in doing so.

The Maine was intact until she was swept of her superstructure in 1920 and what remains of that now

mind anyone diving her, they would object most strongly to anyone taking souvenirs.

Even though thousands of divers had the Maine in their logbooks, it wasn't until 1987, that two divers from Bracknell BSAC, Nick Jewson and Peter Williams, on their first dive on her, found her bell! It is two feet high and five and a half stone of solid brass. All those other divers who missed it since diving on her started in 1961, can take some comfort that it

They found the bell! Left to right, Peter Williams, Nick Jewson. In background Robert Pannell, then Chairman of Torbay Branch. This picture was taken at the official presentation of the Maine's bell to Torbay divers.

lies on the seabed a short distance away from the starboard side of the wreck. There are big congers in the main wreckage. Beware jagged edges; the hull plating is now thin in places. She lies across the tide in strong streams of several knots at springs. It is essential to dive her two hours after high or two-and-a-half hours after low. Latest reports say her counterstern is broken and falling away and her poop deck is collapsing inwards.

Section FIVE.

Dive Sites to the West of the Sound.

Admiralty Charts:
1613 (Eddystone Rocks to Berry Head)
1267 (Falmouth to Plymouth)
1900 (Approaches to Plymouth)

Eddystone Rocks
Depths: To 54m

The Eddystone Lighthouse dominates the skyline for miles around Plymouth from its position nearly nine miles off Rame Head. It is 10 miles from the entrance to Plymouth Sound.

The rocks are made up of three reefs, the Western, Southern, and Northern, and they cover a square mile of seabed. These reefs gives some of the best visibility diving in British waters. Because of that, and the spectacular undersea mountains rising up from 54m in places, it is heavily dived. It is also heavily fished and potted, which has decimated the once thriving crab and lobster population.

The rusty red of the rocks comes from a rare form of granite gneiss, which makes up the three ridges of the main mass of the reef, which is 600 yards long. Upon the central ridge stands the lighthouse. The stump of the old granite lighthouse dating from 1759 is on the western ridge and only 42 yards from the base of the present lighthouse.

The present lighthouse is the fourth. The first, Winstanley's stone and tarred wood building, was completed in 1699 and was destroyed in the Great

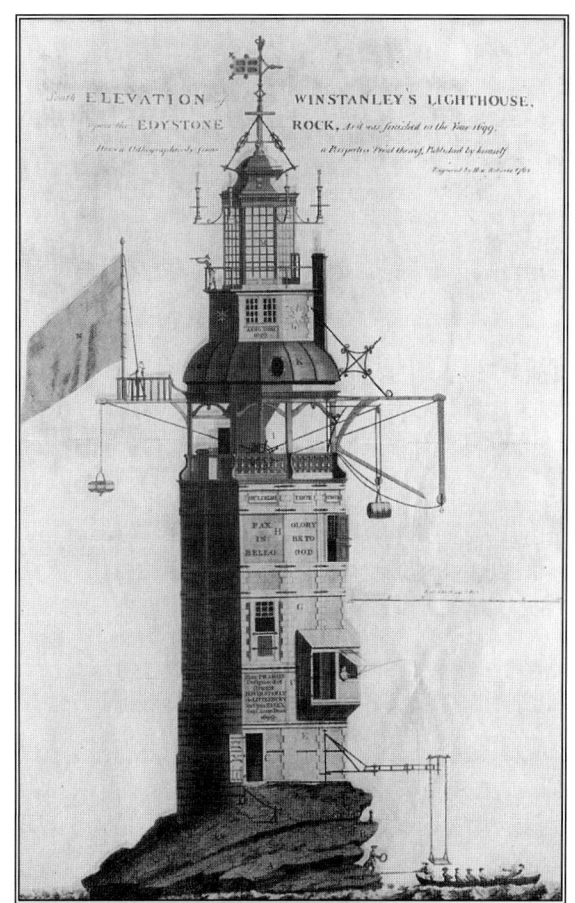

Winstanley's tower, which was to become his tomb, when completed in 1699.

Storm of November 26, 1703, killing Winstanley, who was visiting it, and the keepers.

The second was John Rudyerd's tower of wood and stone, which was destroyed by fire in 1755.

And the third was John Smeaton's stone tower, finished in 1759, which it seems would have been standing there now if the rock had not given way under it. This is the lighthouse whose stump is still on the rock with the upper part re-erected on Plymouth Hoe.

The southern end of the reef gives the steepest drop-offs and the tide is strongest at the tips of the spines. This is where the most marine life is found.

Popular dives are the Pinnacles, which soar up from great depths to within 4m of the surface just off the western end of the reef. The North-East Rock, which just shows at low, is a wonderful sight - its faces are covered with huge veils of white plumose anemones.

The Eddystone gets its name from the constant swirls and eddies in the sea around it. Great gullies run down from the spines to the sandy seabed. Iron work close to the present lighthouse is likely to be debris from the building work from 1878 to 1882.

But there are plenty of wreck remains on and around the Eddystone. The earliest recorded is the Half Moon lost in 1673. Then there was the Snowdrop, lost with all 60 aboard in 1696. About the same time the Constant, owned by Henry Winstanley, hit the Eddystone and sank. It was the loss of this ship which spurred him into building the first lighthouse on the reef in 1698.

Despite the various lighthouses, ships contined to be wrecked on the rocks - the Winchelsea in 1703; the Aire with a cargo of cannon and military stores in 1861 (divers have reported seeing cannon close to the Eddystone); the George Thomas in 1869; the Surprise in 1872; Paulus Heinkes in 1880; Tellus in 1887 and the Lillie in 1894.

Those were all sailing ships. The first steamer to be wrecked was the Hiogo in 1867 (see next entry). Diving round the Eddystone is always turning up the unexpected. In a gully to the north of the reef in 30m, local divers found a huge copper bowl, 6ft in diameter and 2ft deep. One diver described it as "like two giant saucers stuck together with a copper spout poking out - an Aladdin's lamp without a handle". This may have been the oil reservoir for one of the early lighthouse lamps.

Hiogo. Tramp steamer.
Sunk: October 1,1867. Unbelievable stupidity!
Position: Sugar Loaf Rock.
Depth: 18m

The Shoguns and their samurai warriors kept Japan shut off from the West for seven centuries. No Western ships called and if there were any survivors of shipwrecks on those coasts, they were never seen again.

But all that changed when a savage civil war smashed the feudal system of the Shoguns and installed Emperor Mutsuhito as supreme ruler until his death in 1912. During that time he opened Japan to Western ideas and civilisation and it was his signature on a treaty which enabled ships to call at Japanese ports.

British merchants were quick to cash in on this new market and had special ships with Japanese names built for the export trade. Such a ship was the 501-ton Hiogo, named after one of the new ports in Japan and built by Laing's of Sunderland.

When the Hiogo left London on September 28, 1867, bound for Madiera and the Cape and then on to Japan with both goods and passengers, she was commanded by Captain Richard Bainton, a seaman of considerable experience. His second mate, Mr.Henry John Johnson also had years of good seafaring on his record.

On September 30, the Hiogo came abreast of the

Start at 11.45 p.m. and Captain Bainton took this a good time to turn in. Before he did so, he told the Chief Mate that the course was west-north-west and he was to pass this course on to the Second Mate when he took over the deck. At 1 a.m. the Second Mate took over and was told the course. It was a fine clear night with only a light wind. The Eddystone Light could be clearly seen ahead.

For 50 minutes more the Hiogo churned along with the Light getting nearer and nearer. At 1.50 a.m. the Second Mate could stand it no longer. He sent a deckhand down to the Master's cabin to tell him that the Eddystone Light was now bearing north-west-by-west and getting very close. Captain Bainton's answer appeared quite mad. "Don't go too near the Light" was his message.

By now the Second Mate was in a terrible state. The light was almost dead ahead, or perhaps just a portion to port. And it was very, very near, indeed! In fact the whole deck was lit up by it. He waited for another five minutes and then sent the deckhand down to the Master again asking what course he should steer now. The Captain replied: "West-north-west". The Second Mate held the course as directed. It seems incredible that any man could keep the ship heading towards obvious destruction, but that's what the Second Mate did.

In less than another five minutes, the forecastle lookout saw the Eddystone rocks and yelled "Hard-a-port". The ship struck as he shouted. The Hiogo impaled herself on the reef to the north-east of the

How a local artist saw it at the time. The Hiogo has slid backwards into deeper water after trying to ram the lighthouse.

Light which now "shone strongly down on her decks".

Sadly, there is no report of what the Captain said to the Second Mate when he rushed on deck. Nor what the Second Mate said to the Captain.

However, it was, apart from the initial shock, a fairly gentle wrecking. There was no sea to speak of, but the hole in her forepeak was large and water poured in, running through the ship, putting out the boiler fires and collecting at the stern. The weight of water began to pull down the whole of her after part. It was low tide when she struck, but the ship's boat was launched with little difficult and all the six passengers and most of the 27 crew got in.

Distress signals soared into the starlit sky and before the tide was high, Plymouth Pilot Boat No.7 arrived and took off Captain Bainton and the rest of the crew. The rising of the tide lifted her despite the water already inside her, and she slid off into deeper water at the stern, leaving her bow and foremast still above water. All the crew and passengers were landed safely at Plymouth.

The wreck brought some prosperity to Plymouth boatmen, who always were an enterprising group. They soon had "excursion trips" running to see "the Wreck by the Lighthouse". One of those they took out was a local artist who drew the wreck from one of these excursion boats and his drawing is reproduced on the previous page.

The official enquiry was held at Greenwich Police Court on Tuesday, October 15. It didn't take long to come to a decision. The three judges concluded "that the Master was guilty of a default directly contributing to the loss of the ship". They suspended his certificate for 12 calendar months.

As for Mr.Henry John Johnson..."With respect to the mate, considering that he was told to keep clear of the light, his running directly on to a danger so apparent to everyone on board, manifested such utter incompetency to perform the duties of a second mate, that this Court has decided to suspend his certificate for 12 calendar months".

Other reports in local newspapers make it clear that the ship struck a rock called the Sugar Loaf, which fishermen today also call the Shark's Fin. It is just to the north-east of the eastern ridge about 120 yards from the stump of Smeaton's lighthouse (for it was Smeaton's light which originally shone down on her) And it is here that divers find her with the main part of her wreckage on a shallow plateau between that rock and the Lighthouse in 12m.

Kelp usually covers almost everything, but valves and oilers are still to be seen. If you sit on top of the engine block you will be in 8m. Much of the superstructure is left flattened to the bottom. The Hiogo's plates are home to big congers. Her condenser has been blown with explosives and the tubes lie scattered in the kelp.

Hand Deeps
Depth: 7m to 46m

An odd name for a reef of rocks and pinnacles and is said to come from the water over them being only a "hand" deep. This is somewhat of an exaggeration as a hand is used as a measure for a horse's height and reckoned to be four inches! The shallowest parts of the Hand Deeps are in fact 7m below water at low springs. In rough weather there are breakers over them and in fine weather the tide produces large ripples.

The rocks lie three-and-a-half miles to the north-west of the Eddystone and provide excellent scenic diving. The tops are covered in kelp, but below that the rocks, which drop down in a series of ledges, are coated with anemones and Devonshire cup corals.

James Eagan Layne. United States Liberty Ship.
Sunk: March 21,1945. Torpedoed.
Position: 50 19 32N; 04 04 42W. Wreck buoy to seaward.
Depth: 24m.

She might have been called the *USS Frank Sinatra*. Or *The Voice*, which at the time of her launch meant the same thing to the teenage "bobby-soxers" of America.

If she had been named after "Ole Blue Eyes" it wouldn't have made much difference,she would still be the most dived wreck in Britain. Every day that the weather will allow, Fort Bovisand boats run a shuttle service out to this wreck to enable more of Britain's sport divers to put her name in their logbooks.

The wreck of the James Eagan Layne lies in Whitsand Bay, the first bay of Cornwall westward out of Plymouth Sound.

Her story starts on October 23, 1944, which is when her keel was laid in the yard of the Delta Shipbuilding Company in New Orleans. She was to be another Liberty ship.

The Liberty ship programme had started much earlier. In 1940, German U-boats were sinking merchant ships faster than British shipyards could build them. A British mission went to the United States to ask for help in building ships to replace these huge Allied losses and took with them a basic design of a big steamer, not pretty, not fast, but seaworthy and capable of carrying the large cargoes needed to continue the war effort. The Americans agreed.

So the Liberty programme began. But they weren't called Liberty ships at once. In fact, the project got off to a poor start when President Roosevelt announcing the first emergency 200-ship building programme, incautiously called them "dreadful-looking objects". After that the mildest thing they were called was "ugly ducklings". But then Admiral Emory Scott Land, chairman of the United States Maritime Commission, called the ships the "Liberty Fleet". It caught on and overnight the ugly ducklings blossomed into Liberty ships. It was a good name. The Liberty ships saved not only Britain but the civilised world. Without Liberty ships the Allies would have collapsed.

During the war more than 2,700 Liberty ships were built to keep President Roosevelt's promise to give Britain ships which were "built by the mile and chopped off by the yard". To cope with this vast surge in shipbuilding, yards sprang up all over the United States.

One of those yards was that of the Delta Shipbuilding Company of New Orleans. It was a new yard and a new company specially formed in 1941 to cope with the emergency shipbuilding programme. Six slipways were set along a narrow channel leading to the great wide Mississippi and they launched the Liberty ships sideways into it. Soon the Delta yard employed 13,000 people and from its start in 1941 to its close in 1945, they produced 132 Liberty ships, plus 32 Liberty tankers and 24 Liberty colliers.

The James Eagan Layne was No.157 and her hull number was MCE 2831. The Delta yard specialised in 100 per cent welding and that's the way they built her. It took 43 miles of welding to put her together!

Most of the Liberty ships were identical in basic details. The James Eagan Layne, for example, closely followed the original British design. She was 7176 tons gross, 441ft 6ins long overall, had a beam of 57ft. She had two oil-fired boilers and her triple expansion engines were the standard type and built like many others at the Joshua Hendy Ironworks of Sunnyvale, California.

Just 40 days after her keel was laid on October 23, she slid sideways into the waters of that Mississippi creek on December 2,1944. After another 16 days fitting out, she was delivered at 11.35 a.m. Central Time to the U.S.Navigation Co.Inc., who were named as her "operator".

If you think that is a fast time for building a whole ship, the Americans with their gift for speedy production, could do even better. As the war rolled on so the Liberty yards found more and more ways of speeding the ships to sea. For example, they made a major hull alteration in the later ships to put nearly all the crew in a single midships housing. This was not only safer, it also economised on piping, heating and outfitting the crew's quarters. Though these had fridges,steam heating and running water in the cabins, the ships were still austere. They had no radio-direction finders, no fire detection equipment, no emergency diesel generators, nor radios in the four steel lifeboats on each and every ship.

The first Liberty ship, the Patrick Henry (named after the American Revolutionary,who cried "Give me liberty or give me death!") was one of 15 launched on September 27,1941. Those first 15 took 150 days to build, then another 95 to fit out. By 1942 the time to launch was down to 51 days with 7 more for fitting out. And later that year a special assembly effort produced a ship in 10 days with delivery only 5 days later. But the world record was set on November 12,1942 when the Robert E.Peary was built in four days and outfitted in another three!

Man behind this incredible feat was Henry J.Kaiser, who became the king of the mass production of ships. Until the war his main interest in construction had been that of dams. As a result he spoke about the "front" and "backend" of ships. He brought in his dam experts to build the docks, then his construction men to build the ships in them. Only one in 200 of those men had ever seen a shipyard before and a quarter of them had never seen the sea! But without preconceived ideas, they went about shipbuilding using their own ways and revolutionised the industry.

Kaiser's speed of building gave rise to the story of a lady who came to launch a ship. When she stood ready with the bottle in her hand there was no ship in front of her. "Start swinging, lady," said Kaiser, "it'll be there!"

The Liberty ships that the men like Kaiser built served all over the world in all theatres of war. Over 200 were lost, 50 of them, like the James Eagan Layne, on their maiden voyage.

"I name this ship, James Eagan Layne, and may God bless all who sail in her" said Mrs.Marjorie Layne as she swung the bottle to splinter against the bows of Liberty Ship No.157 in New Orleans on the Saturday morning of December 2, 1944.

If there was a sob in her voice it is not surprising. The ship which slid away from her into the muddy waters of the Mississippi was the first ship to be named for a merchant seaman who gave his life in the Second World War. And that seaman, Second Engineer James Eagan Layne, was her husband.

Standing by her side when she christened that ship

LOCAL MAN IS MISSING AFTER TANKER IS SUNK

James E. Layne Believed Lost; Capt. James S. Poche Is Rescued.

One Baton Rougean was listed as missing and another was rescued in the sinking by Axis submarines of two American tankers, according to news dispatches reaching here.

Missing is James E. Layne, second assistant engineer of 2937 Edar street here. Rescued along with 14 men on his tanker was Capt. James S. Poche.

The two tankers were torpedoed off the Atlantic coast April 8 when only three miles apart.

Captain Poche's wife resides here at 829 Basler drive.

Mr. Layne's family lives here. He has been working for the past eight years at the Standard Oil company, and has been shipping out of here on boats during all of that time. He and his wife have been married for the past 18 years, and they have three children: Beverly, 11, J. E. Layne, Jr., 4; and Wallace Lee, 21 months.

His father, Raymond L. Layne, his two brothers, Raymond, and Austin, and his sister, Pauline Layne, all live in Alachua, Fla.

Others Missing.

Among the others listed as missing are Oswald Ryder, messman, Ville Platte; James E. Ott, fireman, Glenmora; Laslie Hange, fireman, Oberlin; and Charlie P. Sistrunk, Mitchell.

Survivors listed included: William D. Beckendorf, first engineer, New Orleans, and James A. Petlow, oiler, Houtsdale.

This was how the New Orleans newspaper reported the death of James Eagan Layne.

was their daughter, 13-year-old Beverley, and left at home in Baton Rouge were James Eagan Layne, Junior, who was seven and Wallace Layne, who was five. Mrs. Layne, the former Marjorie Pinder, had been married to James Eagan Layne for 18 years.

At first all Liberty ships were named after famous people in the history of the United States. This policy was changed after fans of Frank Sinatra plagued the Maritime Commission in Washington with demands for one of the Liberty ships to be called "The Voice". The Commission refused to name a ship after a pair of tonsils and the naming policy was changed in 1944 when it was decided that in future the names of Liberty ships were to be those of merchant seamen who had lost their lives in the present

Delta Ship Honors Seaman Who Died

The S. S. James Eagan Layne, first ship to be named for a merchant seaman who gave his life in the present war, was launched Saturday morning by the Delta Shipbuilding Company, Inc.

The S. S. Layne, one of the 100 Liberty ships which will be built by the local firm which will honor seamen who lost their lives in action, was sponsored by Mrs. J. E. Layne, Baton Rouge, widow of the honored man, who was second assistant engineer on the Esso Baton Rouge, which was torpedoed and sunk on April 8, 1942.

Southern States papers announce the naming of the ship.

war. And so James Eagan Layne became the first merchant seaman to have a Liberty ship named after him.

He had worked for Standard Oil for eight years, regularly crewing the tankers which ran up and down the Atlantic coast of America. He lived at that time at 2937 Edar Street, Baton Rouge, not far from his skipper, Captain James S. Poche of Basler Drive, who commanded the Esso Baton Rouge. Layne was second assistant engineer on that tanker.

He was 39 when the Esso Baton Rouge left New Orleans, and headed west, giving the Dry Tortugas at the tip of the Florida Keys a wide berth, before heading north up the East Coast of the States for her home port of Wilmington, North Carolina. Waiting for her were the U-boats.

The German submarines were close in to the American coast on the orders of Admiral Karl Donitz,

Commander in Chief of Germany's submarines, who was determined to cripple the Liberty ship programme. He believed that the way to do this was to sink the American tankers, which carried oil from the Gulf of Mexico to the Liberty shipyards, many of which were on the East coast. At first the U-boats found it easy killing. From January 15 to May 10,1942, they claimed to have sunk 112 tankers totalling 927,000 tons. But it wasn't enough to brake the high-speed building of Liberty ships.

Early in the morning of April 8, 1942, U-123, commanded by Kapitan-leutnant Reinhard Hardegen, spotted two tankers off Brunswick,Georgia. Hardegen, a young, but veteran submariner and already holder of the Knight's Cross with Oak Leaves, knew he had nothing to fear from the tankers (convoys were to come later) and at 7 a.m. torpedoed the 9264-ton Oklahoma, also of Wilmington, and then, having let her crew take to the boats, surfaced and put five rounds into her from his 10.5cm deck gun. Seeing that she appeared to be sinking, he then set off after the Esso Baton Rouge which was now heading at full speed for the coast. At 7.15 a.m. Hardegen caught up and his torpedo struck the tanker between the engine room and the bunkers on the starboard side. It was this torpedo which killed Second Engineer James Eagan Layne, Fireman William I.Schatch and Oiler Carl B.Hollger. Captain Poche and the rest of the crew of 37 were saved.

By now U.S. Navy ships were approaching and Hardegen took U-123 down and away. He later reported both tankers as sunk. In fact both were beached and were salvaged and both were sunk again by U-boats later in the war!

At the beginning of March,1945, three months after the s.s. James Eagan Layne was launched, she steamed across the Atlantic on her maiden voyage. Her holds were crammed with war supplies, lorries, jeeps, railway rolling stock, and tank parts. On arrival at Barry Roads, she was attached to coastal convoy BTC 103 and moved off towards her final destination which was to be Ghent.

The Allies were on the rampage through Europe. The Russians were racing for Berlin through East Prussia. Britain's Coldstream Guards broke the German paratroopers' line on the Wesel bridgehead in a bloody fight with bayonets. And Patton's US Third Army tanks were rolling forward in a mad dash to reach the Rhine at Ludwigshafen. The James Eagan Layne's cargo of Sherman tank spares was urgently needed if Patton's tanks were to keep up the pace.

But at 3.40 in the foggy afternoon of March 21,1945, Kapitan-leutnant Ernst Cordes in U-1195 found the convoy. We don't know why he picked the James Eagan Layne as his target, though she was the lead ship of the second column in the convoy and presumably highly visible. We do know that shortly before four o'clock he sent one torpedo into her. It struck on the starboard side behind her engine room. She lost all power immediately and swished to a halt on the calm sea. Her crew tensed, waiting for Cordes' second torpedo, but it never came. He may have lost his victim in the fog or dived deep to avoid the convoy's escorts, which moved in fast, depth-charging all likely echoes in the area.

After a few minutes the James Eagan Layne appeared to be sinking and Captain William Sleek ordered "abandon ship".He and his crew of 42 and the 27 U.S.Navy gunners, who manned the four gun emplacements (bow, stern and one either side of the bridge),all got off safely.

Two Admiralty tugs, HMS Flaunt and HMS Atlas were soon on the scene. As the Liberty ship had now steadied on an even keel.and seemed likely to remain afloat for some time despite flooding of both rear holds and her engine room, it was decided to tow her to Falmouth, rather than the nearer port of Plymouth. Captain Sleek, his chief engineer and one of the crew reboarded her for the tow. Shortly after the tow started, the Plymouth lifeboat arrived, but by the time they got there it was clear that the James Eagan Layne was not going to make Falmouth.

One of the lifeboat crew at the time, Mr.W.F.Lillicrap, of Mutley, described her then as "awash to her decks and clearly in danger of sinking". It was then decided to try and beach her in Whitsand Bay.

The tugs did well to get her there. But they finally made it and she settled to the sandy bottom a mile from Rame Head at 10.30pm that night. Only the tops of her three masts showed above water.

Some salvage started almost at once. Her guns were taken out and any U.S.Army equipment,which could be easily reached was lifted out of her holds. The tank spares were not salved in time to affect the course of the war. In 1952, the United States Government sold the ship to an Icelandic firm - "to completely dismantle the hull", but her new owners failed to complete that contract though some small salvage took place on May 12,1953. By then only No.2 mast still showed, complete with cross-trees. In October, 1967, a British firm salved her prop, condenser and prop shaft. Some time during this period her standing mast was cut down to a 21ft stump, but it still provided a good mooring point for dive boats. However in January, 1973, even that collapsed after a storm. After that only the big wreck buoy marked her grave.

More than fifty years is a long time for a ship to remain ship-shaped underwater in such comparatively shallow water. The fact that this Liberty ship has survived so long is a tribute to the workmanship of the men who built her in New Orleans all those years ago.

However, those who have dived her very recently fear that her days as a ship-like ship are numbered. Ground swell damage after each storm is becoming more and more obvious. A year...five years...who can tell how long she will remain such an excellent dive?

But, however long she lasts, she has proved a fine memorial to Second Engineer James Eagan Layne and all the other American merchant seamen who died in World War Two. Perhaps most of all she has been a constant reminder of the United States' dedication to Britain's liberty in World War Two.

There are great sights in wreck diving near Bovisand. Sitting on the seabed at 22m and looking up at the James Eagan Layne's bow hanging out over you is certainly one of them. This, in good visibility, makes the perfect start to a tour of the ship. At the top of the bow in 10m it is easy to see signs of recent change. The forecastle is collapsing in on itself and the anchorwinches which used to be clear on the bow have fallen down into the forecastle. The chain locker is still there and the diver can see where the chain ran out to the hawse holes.

Further back a cargo winch has now fallen into No.1 hold. On the starboard side of this hold and No.2 and No.3, in fact right back to the engine room, there are sections of the plating which have broken away. So much has fallen that it tends to look as though the whole side has dropped to the seabed. This starboard side break up ahead of the engine room is worse than on the port side of the wreck.

It is possible to swim from Hold No.1 to Hold No.2 with no difficulty. It is in this area that there are large numbers of wheels from the railway rolling stock being carried to Europe to replace the huge amount destroyed by Allied air sweeps prior to the Invasion. Here the decking has fallen in leaving the ribs intact together with the deck frames.

Tony Hillgrove, a veteran Fort Bovisand diving instructor, has dived the ship more than most people. He says that access to the main engine used to be simple from Hold No.3 just ahead of it, but now the decking has fallen in on top. As the sides of the engine room are also collapsing, access to the actual engine is now almost impossible for the average diver on the wreck.

The big open area behind the engine room is really No4 hold. It doesn't look much like a hold any more with big piles of rubble. Ladders lie across them and wire tangles around. Agricultural machinery was stowed here and seed drills and pickaxe heads and water pipe couplings can be seen poking up out of the debris. All this part of the cargo was intended to help war-shattered Europe start feeding herself again.

The ship is broken by No.5 hold and the last 30feet of stern lie a short distance away. Before leaving the main wreckage to find it, take a look at the port side. It is a marvellous sight - a vast sheet of white anemones and deadmen's fingers, which almost glow at you. Here too hang a huge shoal of horse mackerel.

The growth and fish life on this part of the wreck is due to the fact that the flood tide goes in and around Whitsand Bay and out to Plymouth, bringing food to the port side as the ship then straddles the tide.

To find the missing stern section, swim out and away from No.5 hold to the south along the bottom for about 15 metres. When the sand gives way to a dark mass of shell and shingle, turn west for another 20 metres and the stern looms up at you.

It lies on its starboard side and is covered with marine growth. The decking has fallen in. But she only recently gave up another part of her cargo. Divers recovered sixty 5.5inch brass shellcases from a compartment under the gun, which once sat on a platform at the stern and had its own ammunition hoist.

Footnote: Though Cordes escaped the depth-charges that day, he was not so lucky further up the Channel 16 days later when he torpedoed the liner Cuba, which was carrying troops from Le Havre to Southampton on April 6,1945. Her escorts hunted U-1195 through the shallow waters and,even though he tried lying silent in 30m, he and his crew of 34 were obliterated by a rain of depth-charges, one of which blew a 20-foot wide hole right beside the conning-tower.

A-7. H.M.Submarine.
Sunk: January 16,1914.   Stuck in the mud?
Position: 50 18 21N; 04 17 52W
Depth: 40m

Why this 99ft-long submarine failed to resurface during exercises in Whitsand Bay on January 16, 1914 is unlikely ever to be known. Naval experts of the time believed that she dived heavily to the seabed and was literally stuck in the mud. There may also have been a leak of the main hatch, which would mean that the 180-ton A-7, built by Vickers in 1904-5, was already full of water when she struck the bottom.

Commanded by Lieutenant G.M.Welman, the sub was carrying out dummy torpedo attacks on HMS Pigmy together with five other submarines. There were reports of bubbles bursting on the surface after A-7 had failed to reappear.

Despite this knowledge of her position, it took Navy salvage crews six days to locate her. When Navy divers went down they found her with her stern buried in deep mud. Attempts to tidal lift her failed to get her off the seabed, and she was left with her nine-man crew still inside her.

Today the A-7 is upright and level with her bows towards the shore and her upper parts clear of the mud. Her conning-tower and periscope are intact.
WARNING: This wreck is bound to be listed under the Military Remains Act as a war grave (see dive planning earlier).

Rosehill. Armed Collier.
Sunk: September 23, 1917. Red-nosed torpedo.
Position: 50 19 40N; 04 18 25W.
Depth: 33m.

Not many captains have lived to tell of seeing the nose of a torpedo before it sank their ship, but Captain Phillip Jones of the Rosehill was one of those few. He saw the torpedo clearly before it blew a great hole in his ship's starboard side just behind the engine room in No.3 hold - and he said that its nose was painted a bright red!

That torpedo was fired by UB-40, commanded by Oberleutnant Howaldt, when the 2788-ton Rosehill was three miles north-west by west of Rame Head, carrying 3980 tons of coal from Cardiff for Devonport. The Rosehill's stern sank down ten feet and Captain Jones, thinking she was going, ordered his crew of 24 to the boats. An hour later the ship didn't appear to be sinking anymore and the entire crew, plus the two gunners for her 12pdr Japanese gun, volunteered to go back aboard. Captain Jones chose the Mate, Second Mate, Chief Engineer, four seamen and two firemen to accompany him when he re-boarded the vessel. After a brief examination they found that most of the ship was dry and the bulkheads looked like holding in the flooded compartments.

Two tugs arrived from Fowey and decided to tow her to Fowey, but made little headway. Then Admiralty tugs called Woonda and Atalanta took over the tow and made for Plymouth.

At 1.50 a.m. the next morning, the ship showed signs of breaking in two and everyone aboard took to the boats. They only just pulled clear before she foundered in Whitsand Bay.

Today she is in 33m, on a sandy seabed, fairly intact, but with a big break towards the stern, from which her big gun has been removed.